# The Politics of Capital Investment

the

# POLITICS

*of*

# CAPITAL INVESTMENT

## The Case of Philadelphia

Carolyn Teich Adams

STATE UNIVERSITY OF NEW YORK PRESS

Published by
State University of New York Press, Albany

©1988 State University of New York




For information, address State University of New York
Press, State University Plaza, Albany, N.Y., 12246

**Library of Congress Cataloging-in-Publication Data**
Adams, Carolyn Teich.
    The politics of capital investment.

    (SUNY series in urban public policy)
    Bibliography: p.
    Includes index.
    1. Capital budget—Pennsylvania—Philadelphia.
2. Capital investments—Pennsylvania—Philadelphia.
3. Urban Policy—Pennsylvania—Philadelphia.    I. Title.
II. Series: SUNY series on urban public policy.
HJ9307.P4A63    1988        336′.014′74811        88–2274
ISBN   0–88706–847–2
ISBN   0–88706–848–0 (pbk.)

# Contents

# Acknowledgments

I am pleased to acknowledge the contribution to this work made by Temple University, whose grant of a study leave enabled me to undertake the research. I also express my appreciation to Barbara Kaplan, Executive Director of the Philadelphia City Planning Commission, for her informed reading of early drafts, and to Mark Mattson of Temple University's Cartography Laboratory, for the fine maps and graphs that appear in this book.

# 1

# Introduction

AMERICA'S cities have shown a resilience in the 1980s that has surprised many long-time observers. The recent boom in office construction has created gleaming new blocks in the hearts of many aging cities, and the economic resurgence of the mid-1980s has replaced many of the lost manufacturing jobs with jobs in service industries.

These signs of urban resurgence, however welcome, are not without their drawbacks. They raise serious questions about how widely the benefits of the current boom will be shared. The fact that the central business districts of many large cities have staged a comeback does not mean that neighborhood revitalization must follow. Because of the segmented nature of both labor markets and housing markets in urban areas, downtown development need not spill over into surrounding neighborhoods. Even as our city centers regain their vitality, nearby residential communities continue to decline.

Some analysts have, in fact, linked the decline of inner city neighborhoods directly to downtown redevelopment.[1] Precisely the same forces that have fed downtown dynamism, they argue, have drained the neighborhoods of their employment base, their shops and services, and their more affluent residents. Chief among the forces contributing to this zero-sum game are government redevelopment programs that concentrate public investments in central business districts, allowing neighborhood facilities to deteriorate. For many urbanists, the issue of public investment in cities is therefore formulated in terms of downtown versus neighborhoods.

Yet not all city neighborhoods suffer the same fate. After decades of study, we continue to search for the reasons why some deteriorate while others remain viable residential communities. What factors determine a neighborhood's vitality? In this study I examine one factor that is widely viewed as contributing to neighborhood growth and stability: public facilities. Local government expenditures for public amenities such as schools, libraries, parks, and recreation centers represent one of the few tools at the disposal of public officials seeking to influence patterns of private investment that shape urban neighborhoods, particularly now that government subsidies for low- and moderate-income housing have almost disappeared. Yet, interestingly, there is little research on the financing and construction of such facilities or their impact on neighborhood change.

Using Philadelphia as a case study, I shall examine municipal spending for the construction of such neighborhood amenities, concentrating particularly on their distribution across neighborhoods and the political elements that have produced that pattern. My second, and equally important, concern is the competition pitting neighborhoods against downtown for the city's limited investment dollars. As they watch neighborhood facilities deteriorate at the same time that new convention centers, sports complexes, and other public projects are being built in the city center, most observers attribute the imbalance to the political clout of downtown business groups. I shall argue instead that the outcome of that competition can be explained as much by the structure of capital markets as by the relative political strength of various factions within the city.


## MODELS OF NEIGHBORHOOD CHANGE

For at least the past twenty-five years urbanists have been alternately horrified and fascinated by the process of urban decay. The dramatic population losses suffered by the aging cities of the northeast and midwest in the period after World War II spawned a whole new lexicon of images to describe the central city, including "wasteland," "doughnut," and "bombed-out war zone." The common theme in this postwar urban imagery is the belief that urban life is gradually receding from our inner cities, as residents and business owners flee from the advancing blight, the deteriorating services, and the social pathologies associated with "dying" neighborhoods. The presence of thousands of abandoned structures and vacant lots in the inner city is seen by many as a sign that large areas will eventually empty out altogether. Even as they lament the passing of older neighborhoods, many planners and politicians talk optimistically about the opportunities presented by this widespread evacuation of land close to the downtown centers. After all, such land can sometimes be profitably redeveloped for middle-income residents, for commercial or institutional uses, or even as recreational space for city dwellers. Many, perhaps even most, urban observers view this process of inner city decay as natural and inevitable.

To a great extent these observers' expectations concerning the future of America's inner cities are based on the pervasive idea of the neighborhood life cycle, a corollary of the spatial models that have traditionally been used to describe the socioeconomic structure of cities. As early as the 1920s and 1930s members of the Chicago School of urban sociology had observed the relationships between the growth of metropolitan areas and the process of neighborhood change. They watched the expanding suburbs draw higher-status households away from the congested urban core and into new "high-grade" residential districts. As once-fashionable neighborhoods were abandoned by their original inhabitants, the housing stock "filtered down" to residents of successively lower socioeconomic status.

The early work of the human ecologists done at the University of Chicago had a mechanistic quality that has pervaded urban spatial analysis all the way to the present day. Urban neighborhoods were thought to follow a common progression, much like the patterns of growth and decay observed in the world of nature. The competition for space among residents with different levels of resources meant that neighborhoods were almost always undergoing transitions of one kind or another. Stasis was simply not permitted, either by nature or by the urban land market.

Classical human ecologists like Ernest Burgess wrote about the process of invasion and succession that resulted when new immigrant groups moved up the economic ladder and into new areas of the city. Beginning in the 1960s scholars began focusing on the movement of blacks into new sections of the metropolis. The recent growth of Hispanic and Asian communities has prompted more research on the residential patterns of these new immigrant groups. But whatever the ethnic or social identity of the group being studied, researchers have continued to rely on the invasion/succession model to explain changes in the condition of the housing stock. When incoming residents have lower incomes than the families they are replacing, a decline in the value and condition of housing is seen as inevitable.

Urban researchers have by and large agreed, not just on the dynamics of the filtering process, but even on the major historical stages by which that process occurs. In a classic analysis published in 1959,[2] Hoover and Vernon set forth the five stages through which most urban neighborhoods can be expected to progress: (1) residential development in single- family dwellings, (2) increasing density with new construction of multifamily units, (3) downgrading of existing structures by conversion to higher-density use, (4) thinning out of the area due to outmigration and reduced household size, and (5) clearance of the land in preparation for renewal. In the early 1970s David Birch worked on quantifying these stages of development,[3] and in the mid-1970s a widely circulated HUD policy paper entitled "The Dynamics of Neighborhood Change"[4] redefined five stages of neighborhood change in terms that were different from, but clearly related to, those used by Hoover and Vernon (healthy, incipient decline, clearly declining, accelerating decline, and abandoned).

Underlying all of these formulations of a neighborhood life cycle is the assumption that the primary determinant of housing conditions and housing values is consumer choice operating in the housing market. That is, the ability and willingness of households to pay for housing determines the desirability, and hence the value, of different housing types and neighborhoods. When a neighborhood's residents are no longer willing to invest in their properties, values decline, making the area attractive to lower socioeconomic groups, who in turn pay lower rents. Given the dominance of the life-cycle model in the urban literature, it is hardly surprising that federally sponsored community development programs have emphasized the upgrading of services, public and commercial facilities, and other amenities, so as to make urban neighborhoods more acceptable to current residents and more appealing to potential newcomers.

In contrast to the heavy emphasis placed on consumer demands and preferences in the neighborhood life-cycle model, a new school of urban research has begun to shift attention to the supply of investment capital as the key to neighborhood stability and change. Writing as political economists of the left, David Harvey and others have argued that neighborhood change depends less on the preferences and demands of consumers than on how industrial, financial, and property capitalists decide to move their holdings. While the classical human ecologists attributed the gradual disinvestment from inner cities to thousands of individual decisions by residents and businesses, this newer school traces disinvestment to the actions of a few large institutions, including banks, insurance companies, and real estate developers. Instead of recognizing a "natural" cycle through which all neighborhoods are destined to pass, the new analysis views neighborhood change as occurring unevenly to reflect the strategies adopted by institutions seeking to maximize their returns.

One such strategy is to prefer investments in new construction over investments in existing development. David Harvey has argued that since capital that is invested in urban infrastructure (or the "built environment," in Harvey's terms) becomes devalued over time, investors constantly seek newer, more profitable sites while withdrawing from older sites. Needless to say, the resulting pattern of continuous turnover leads to the decline of existing neighborhoods.[5]

Another strategy is to withhold investments altogether from certain "redlined" sections of the city. Research on the mortgage lending patterns of banks has shown a clear pattern of avoidance of certain neighborhoods, most often those containing large minority populations. By channeling loans away from those areas perceived to carry a higher risk, banks virtually guarantee their decay.

Following David Harvey, other neo-Marxists have borrowed the concept of stages of decline, but redefined the stages to emphasize the movement of capital as the driving force in neighborhood change. According to Naparstek and Cincotta,[6] the first steps in the decline of a healthy neighborhood (their Stage I) are the decisions by lenders to tighten loan requirements for mortgages in the area (Stage II) and eventually to redline the area altogether (Stage III). The lack of conventional mortgage money leads buyers to resort to mortgages insured by the Federal Housing Administration (Stage IV). When defaults occur on FHA-insured properties, they are resold to speculators and absentee landlords whose unwillingness to invest in maintenance and repairs results in deterioration and abandonment (Stage V). Neil Smith labels the five stages differently, but traces the same path toward capital depreciation in the inner city.[7] In these descriptions of the process there is nothing inevitable about the abandonment of neighborhoods; it results from a conscious policy of financial institutions to withdraw from certain sections of the city—a policy based on the self-fulfilling prophecy that these areas are likely to decline in value.

## PUBLIC INVESTMENT IN URBAN NEIGHBORHOODS

In seeking to explain neighborhood change, the neo-Marxists have focused most of their attention on private market investors who furnish capital for builders, landlords, and home owners. Yet the private market is by no means the only investor in urban neighborhoods. Local governments spend very large sums to provide the basic infrastructure that supports development. Public investments in roads, sewer and water systems, parks, libraries, and schools all increase the attractiveness of the land and encourage development by shifting some of its costs to the taxpayers. Suburban governments typically undertake such capital improvements as a way to guide new development within their boundaries. Central cities must constantly renew and upgrade their physical infrastructure to accommodate to the demographic and economic shifts that affect them. Their failure to do so, and the resulting decay in urban public facilities, has emerged as one of the most important policy problems of the 1980s. In particular, the connection between public works and economic productivity has brought the issue of public disinvestment in urban infrastructure to the fore. One widely read account of the problem, with the colorful title *America in Ruins*, describes the damage to economic expansion being done by underinvestment in transportation, utilities, and other networks that underpin all economic activity. The authors conclude that "at least one half of the nation's communities are unable to support modernized development until major new investments are made in their basic facilities that undergird the economy."[8]

For all the concern about the infrastructure problem that is now being expressed by policy makers and policy analysts, little that has been written moves beyond surveying the deteriorating conditions of public facilities and calling for more public investment. We have little information about how public officials go about making investment decisions,[9] and even less about how their decisions affect their communities. This study is an attempt to address those two questions in the context of one major American city, Philadelphia.

I depart from most other recent work on the urban infrastructure problem by focusing more heavily on community facilities than on major infrastructure systems like expressways or utilities. Economists distinguish between public works that directly support the production or movement of private sector goods and services, and those that do not. The former category of facilities is sometimes called "economic overhead capital" (EOC), while the latter is referred to as "social overhead capital" (SOC).[10] Some examples of EOC are roads, bridges, ports, airports, utilities, water and sewer systems, and publicly owned facilities that support entertainment, tourism, and retail activities in the city, such as tourist and convention centers, stadiums, etc. These are the capital items that figured prominently in the Urban Institute's recent series of reports on six American cities' capital programs, and in most other treatments of the infrastructure problem. The category of SOC includes schools, libraries, fire and police stations, recreation, health, and welfare facilities. Note that the criterion for distinguishing between the two categories is not *whether* a particular investment supports the local economy, but rather *how directly* it does so. As many economists have argued, SOC expenditures make an important long-term contribution to economic productivity. School expenditures offer the best example, but other SOC expenditures that improve living conditions for the labor force can also be seen to benefit the economy indirectly. Indeed, one economist has even argued that SOC expenditures are critical to the economic survival of the postindustrial service city:

> Spending on schools, health care, higher education, and the like has come under increasing attack because they are thought to be "wasteful." Yet, upon examination, it appears that [these services] have provided the basic economic infrastructure upon which the post industrial service city has been constructed.[11]

Increasingly, surveys of corporate decision makers have suggested that when they choose a location for a new plant or office, they are concerned about quality-of-life issues, including public services and amenities. As industries become more footloose, they seek a community whose schools, transportation, cultural and recreational facilities will contribute to their employees' standard of living. In economies dominated increasingly by service and information functions, a community's primary asset is the quality of its workforce—a workforce that depends upon public facilities for its education, health, recreation, and welfare.

Political economists writing from a neo-Marxist perspective have argued that in capitalist economies public services have inevitably assumed a growing significance, as the cost of reproducing labor power became increasingly socialized. More and more, the costs of services and facilities required to maintain a productive workforce have been borne collectively by taxpayers rather than by businesses alone. The demand for changing employment skills required education and training; working families required support in caring for children, the elderly, and disabled; physical and emotional stresses at the workplace brought about a need for health care and recreational opportunities. Rather than supplying these services directly or paying workers enough to buy such services on the private market, capitalists looked to government as a provider.

This observation of growing government intervention in health, education, transportation and housing has led Manuel Castells and other neo-Marxist scholars to explain the heightened political dissatisfaction with local government since the 1960s as an expression of consumer complaints. They reason that as government (especially municipal government) emerged as a more visible agent delivering these various services, public authorities were increasingly held responsible for various distributive effects which consumers had previously accepted as the natural and inevitable outcomes of market forces. Lower income citizens became especially vocal, since they depended more heavily on public services than did middle-class residents. When they were not adequately served, they blamed government.[12]


## DISCRIMINATION AGAINST POOR NEIGHBORHOODS

One of the main issues to be tackled in this study is the city's record of allocating social overhead capital among its neighborhoods. I am especially interested in how capital planners in postwar Philadelphia have treated the poor and minority areas of the city, relative to the better-off neighborhoods. The answer to this question may seem so obvious to some of my readers that they will wonder why I bother to ask it.

At least since the Kerner Commission report of 1968, urban observers have by and large accepted the view that part of the blame for the deteriorating conditions in our inner city must be shared by public authorities who have withheld services and investments from those areas. As middle-class residents have left their old neighborhoods behind, those districts have increasingly been neglected by municipal departments, with the result that the residents must suffer the effects of both private and public disinvestment at the same time. One of the most succinct descriptions of the process is that supplied by economist Daniel Fusfeld:

Local governments throughout the country have allowed their investments in poverty districts to fall by not replacing depreciation of buildings and other investments. Schools and libraries have been allowed to deteriorate, parks to run down, streets and curbs to go unrepaired, fire and police stations to depreciate, and medical facilities to deteriorate. In part, this process is due to the added strains that a denser population has placed on public facilities. . . . However, in part, it is due to the traditional tendency of city governments to maintain facilities in the middle- and upper-income areas and to put the priorities of the slums last.[13]

What are the reasons for this public neglect of poor neighborhoods? Many explanations have been offered, most of which fall into three main categories. The first is based on an interpretation of urban politics as a pluralist system in which innumerable groups compete for the resources of city government. Their relative success depends on how coalitions form in various issue-areas, and how much political clout the coalition members wield. The key consideration for any interest group to "get in the game" is the strength and reliability of its power base. According to this view, poor neighborhoods have fewer political resources and, hence, they lose out in the competition for municipal services and investments. Low-income, minority neighborhoods suffer politically from a double liability.

Racism in the housing markets of most cities has led to the concentration of blacks in certain neighborhoods where city services have been traditionally inferior to the services delivered to whites. Although the Supreme Court struck down the practice of providing "separate but equal" facilities thirty years ago, the spatial separation between blacks and whites in American cities makes it extremely difficult to insure that public authorities supply equivalent services to all races. Indeed, on several occasions during the 1970s the nation's courts declared local governments to be illegally discriminating against minority sections of the community in their provision of public services. Most often, the equal protection clause of the Fourteenth Amendment was cited as the basis for protecting black neighborhoods against such unfavorable treatment. While the courts have been restrained and sometimes contradictory in their rulings regarding unequal service distribution,[14] the publicity surrounding these cases has confirmed the widespread assumption that the powerlessness of poor minority residents accounts for the inadequate facilities and services in their neighborhoods.

The theory that low-income minority neighborhoods receive fewer public goods because they lack political clout squares with our knowledge about the political behavior of low-income populations. Survey research has shown that the likelihood of voting declines as incomes declines, and that similar patterns exist for other kinds of political participation (e.g., attending meetings and demonstrations, working on campaigns). Knowing that low-income groups are less politically active than middle-income groups, pluralists assume that the price they pay for political apathy is fewer parks and pools and less efficient trash pickup and street maintenance than are provided to neighborhoods with strong political organizations.

Bernard Frieden and Marshall Kaplan, for example, made use of pluralist theory to explain why decades of federal subsidies for local public works have made so little impact in poverty areas. A lack of political power, they argued, has consistently prevented poor neighborhoods from getting their share of federal funds. They characterized the Model Cities program of the 1960s as the only recent instance of a sizable federal program targeted directly at poverty areas, but noted that because of Model Cities' emphasis on services rather than bricks-and-mortar, Model Cities did very little to improve public facilities. Frieden and Kaplan summed up the no-win situation for poverty neighborhoods this way:

> During the thirties, they were unable to get their share of public works funds for street improvements, playgrounds, and swimming pools because they lacked political clout at the local level and because Federal funds did not give them special priority.
>
> During the sixties, when Federal requirements worked in their favor and funds were available, hardware improvements went out of style. Instead, the money went for a diffuse range of public service activities such as educational and manpower projects that were most fashionable because they were seriously innovative, experimental, and ambitious. However, they were also high risks in terms of community facilities.
>
> Today, hardware expenditures are again fashionable; but in many areas the poor lack the political clout to get the facilities they want, and there are no Federal programs to send money directly into their neighborhoods. When will they ever get their parks, playgrounds, and swimming pools?[15]

Needless to say, pluralists use the same reasoning to explain why affluent white areas of the city get more than their share of public resources. Their money and their reputation for higher voter turnout give them the edge in political competition with their less affluent neighbors. Thus, in constructing a bond issue to go before the voters for support of new facilities, city officials can be expected to include projects that benefit the higher-income sections of the city regardless of the relative urgency of those projects, simply because they need the support of those areas in order to win.

An altogether different view is taken by the neo-Marxist school of urban analysis mentioned earlier in this chapter. Rapidly developing in both Western Europe and the United States, this new school includes such theorists as Manuel Castells in France, Michael Harloe in Britain, and David Harvey in the United States.[16] As would be the case with any emerging school of analysis, the participants in its development are far from agreeing on all points of the analysis, but they do share a general view of urban politics that is in sharp conflict with pluralist theory. Rather than seeing local government as an arena in which changing coalitions dominate at different times and on different issues, the neo-Marxists view government activity as broadly determined by the relations of production in society. Municipal policy, they believe, consistently reflects the needs of industrial capital (e.g., manufacturing firms), finance capital (e.g., banks), and major land owners, rather than the needs and preferences of local voters.

What are those needs? On the one hand, capitalists need to have local government operate in a way that protects and encourages capital accumulation, by regulating land use for the benefit of developers and investors, by supplying transportation, utilities and other infrastructure for commerce and industry, and by maintaining a level of public order and safety that permits businesses to flourish. As one observer has put it:

> The inexorable logic of capitalism forces owners to do whatever is in their power to gain profit so that it can be reinvested so as to gain still more profit so that it can be reinvested and so on in a never-ending cycle. . . . Profit maximization and capital accumulation is therefore the over- riding goal of owners of capital. . . . Accordingly, owners as a class must seek to organize society and more specifically urban space in order to enhance profit maximization.[17]

On the other hand, city governments also perform an array of social welfare functions designed to mitigate the social costs of the accumulation process. It is these public welfare functions that draw the most support from workers. The tension between these two major functions is, therefore, a reflection of the tension between the two classes, and it is at the heart of local political struggles, according to the neo-Marxists. Nowhere is this tension more apparent than when municipalities must borrow. Because banks and other financial institutions control the city's access to loans, they have significant influence over public policy. The more urgent is the politicians' need to borrow, the more leverage is available to those who control capital. Witness the role the banks have played in forcing service cutbacks in cities where they have been called upon to bail out municipal governments or school districts on the verge of bankruptcy.

James O'Connor's *Fiscal Crisis of the State*, published in 1973, laid the groundwork for much of the recent analysis emphasizing the influences of economic structures on policy. O'Connor distinguished three basic types of public expenditures. The first is "social investment," which is equivalent to expenditures on what I referred to earlier as economic overhead capital—that is, expenditures on roads, bridges, ports, utility lines, and other items that directly support private sector productivity. O'Connor's second and third types are both cases of our earlier category of social overhead capital, for within this general rubric O'Connor distinguishes between outlays for "social consumption" and those for "social expenses." The former are outlays for facilities or services that bring down the cost of reproducing labor. In simplest terms, the government supplements the wages paid by employers with a "social wage," consisting of basic services needed by workers in order to remain productive in their jobs. These include schools, public health and safety, recreational opportunities, etc. By providing these public services, government enables employers to pay a lower wage than they would otherwise have to pay, and thus protects capitalism from the real costs of its production.

O'Connor's category of "social expenses," on the other hand, denotes outlays that are aimed, not at bolstering productivity and profits, but rather at maintaining social peace by ameliorating some of the social damage that is the inevitable by-product of capitalism. Here, we are talking mainly about programs for the unemployed or underemployed—for example, income support programs of all kinds, drug abuse or mental health clinics, nutrition programs for indigent mothers and infants, and shelters for the homeless. Needless to say, these categories often overlap. O'Connor himself pointed out that "nearly every state (i.e., governmental) expenditure is part social investment, part social consumption, and part social expense."[18]

Nevertheless, O'Connor's categories have proved useful to other like-minded writers, who have observed a gradual shift in local government expenditures in inner city neighborhoods away from the first two categories, and toward the third. As larger and larger segments of the inner city population have become marginal to the labor force, public authorities have withdrawn from their neighborhoods the types of investments that are intended to contribute, either directly or indirectly, to productivity. What these neighborhoods have received instead are shelters, clinics, halfway houses, and drop-in centers that provide ameliorative welfare services. Their function is to keep the peace rather than to integrate the inner city population into the economic mainstream.

> Since World War II environmental resources in white-collar and even some blue collar neighborhoods have been greatly improved, to provide the more educated, more "cultured" labor supplies needed . . . while the slums . . . have been neglected, because of stagnation in the demand for their labor. . . . Lower class areas are thus deprived of the money needed to provide the high levels of health, education, and skill of middle class areas. They are internal reservations for the reserve army of the barely employed.[19]

Yet a third perspective on the neglect of inner city neighborhoods is based on the observation that city officials frequently use allocation strategies that maximize their ability to show results, even if it means spending money on the not-so-needy. In the human services field, this strategy is known as "creaming," or selecting from the pool of applicants those who are likely to show the greatest improvement as a result of receiving the service, rather than those who demonstrate the greatest need for it.

In the case of physical renewal and redevelopment programs, an investment strategy that bypasses the worst neighborhoods in favor of those that seem more easily salvaged has come to be labeled "triage." To operate with this decision-making model, city officials must first classify city neighborhoods, according to whether they are:

1. Able to maintain themselves as viable communities mainly through private initiative and investment, without much public investment
2. Capable of improving and sustaining themselves only with some infusions of public aid
3. Deteriorated so far that they are incapable of recovery, even with massive public investment

Officials then gradually withdraw capital investments from the neighborhoods in the third category, in order to concentrate their limited resources on areas that are potentially restorable. In the interim, residents remaining in the poorest neighborhoods continue to receive social services, until they can be relocated into other parts of the city. Note the difference between this model and the pluralist model: here, the city official who decides to withhold investment from a blighted neighborhood is not necessarily calculating political gains and losses. Rather, he or she is making a rational judgment that further public investment will yield no significant physical or economic improvement in that neighborhood, and that systematic disinvestment is therefore the only reasonable alternative, given limited funds.

Needless to say, this model presents a highly controversial interpretation of the community development process. It is praised by its proponents as the only sensible means of allocating scarce resources, while it is castigated as inhumane by its critics.

Although the controversy over triage surfaced only in the mid-1970s, the concept was well known even in the early years of urban renewal. For example, a classic statement of the strategy is to be found in a 1956 report on Philadelphia's urban renewal program, which concluded that the standard practice of targeting the worst neighborhoods first was simply unworkable. It recommended instead that redevelopment officials divide the city's renewal areas into three categories; "A" areas (most deteriorated), "B" areas (moderately deteriorated), and "C" areas (least deteriorated). (Note that this scheme presumed a fourth category consisting of those neighborhoods that had not been included among the renewal areas because they were in good condition.) Funds should be concentrated, the report argued, in the "C," or least deteriorated, areas because that was where the city could have the greatest impact.[20]

The triage controversy erupted in the mid-1970s when Anthony Downs advocated the triage strategy in a monograph that he based on a series of training workshops that his consulting firm had done for the Department of Housing and Urban Development. Downs contended that cities needed some principles by which to target the limited funds available under the Community Development Block Grant program, and he recommended triage as the best available alternative.[21] Shortly after Downs published this recommendation, a Brookings Institution survey of twenty-seven sample cities found evidence that a modified triage strategy was indeed being used in cities across the country.[22]

I have dwelt on these three explanatory frameworks at some length, in order to show just how widespread is the consensus among urban observers that the poorest neighborhoods of our cities, especially those containing high concentrations of minority households, do not get their share of public improvements. Each of the perspectives outlined above has a different answer to the question: Why? But all of them take as given that public authorities discriminate against disadvantaged neighborhoods. It should be said that each of these frameworks concedes the possibility, under special circumstances, that local government may temporarily depart from its normal pattern and allocate increased resources to poor and minority communities. Most pluralists would admit that even a disadvantaged community can sometimes gain leverage over local government resources by aligning itself with more powerful groups in the city, as when a poor neighborhood manages to secure community improvements as part of a larger redevelopment scheme, or by threatening serious disruption. For example, many city governments responded to the racial outbreaks of the 1960s by temporarily expanding their assistance to black communities. Similarly, neo-Marxists would acknowledge that the economic elites, whose interests dominate local policy making, have occasionally responded to political protests with temporary concessions, and have provided on a permanent basis some ameliorative benefits and services to sustain the economically marginal residents of the city. Such concessions, however, are exceptions to the long-term pattern of discrimination that is seen as a fact of urban life.

## EXAMINING POLICY OUTCOMES

The reader will have noticed that each of the frameworks outlined above focuses on the policy-making process—that is, on how public policies are made and who dominates. If we now turn from the literature on the policy making process to the literature on policy outcomes, we find a good deal more disagreement over whether local governments systematically discriminate against poor and minority communities.

During the 1970s, researchers began to use quantitative techniques to relate the distribution of municipal expenditures to such factors as neighborhood income level, racial composition, and political power. In 1974 Levy et al. found in Oakland that while expenditures for libraries and street-resurfacing favored the well-to-do areas, the pattern of school expenditures formed a U-shaped curve, with the best-off and worst-off neighborhoods getting proportionately more resources than the middle-income areas.[23] When Lineberry examined a range of services in San Antonio, he discovered that for police patrols, there was relatively little variation in the city's allocations from area to area. For other services, particularly those delivered at fixed sites, there was significant variation among neighborhoods, but it could not be shown to be related to racial or income characteristics. The one pattern that Lineberry did perceive was that the older, more densely populated neighborhoods of the city appeared to get larger allocations than did the newer districts.[24] In Detroit, Jones et al.[25] found that a favorable response from city agencies was more a result of citizen-initiated contacts than of any particular set of neighborhood characteristics. In Chicago,[26] Mladenka came to the surprising conclusion that there was no positive association between a ward's vote for the Democratic political machine and its share of the city's expenditures for park, fire, and sanitation services. Yet another big-city study, that done by Boyle and Jacobs for New York City,[27] showed that expenditures for health, education, and welfare services favored poor neighborhoods, while services to property favored the neighborhoods making the largest tax contributions per capita. And the authors of one recent analysis of police expenditures in the neighborhoods of Boston cautioned that it is premature to reject the underclass hypothesis; they found some evidence that both racial composition and political clout influenced a neighborhood's share of the resources.[28] Summing up the available research findings on expenditure outcomes, Richard Rich cautioned that

> the evidence provides no clear basis for either accepting or rejecting hypotheses about overall patterns in the distribution of public services or for assessing the performance of urban government in general with respect to the equitable provision of services.[29]

Such caution is especially appropriate when the subject is capital improvements, as opposed to services. Because so little research has been done to date on neighborhood facilities, it is difficult to know which pattern we are more likely to see in Philadelphia's postwar capital program: systematic discrimination against poor and black neighborhoods, as is presumed by so many urban theorists, or unpatterned variations among neighborhoods, as is suggested by recent empirical research on municipal operating expenditures. Chapter 3 addresses this question directly.

## HOW IMPORTANT ARE CAPITAL IMPROVEMENTS TO NEIGHBORHOODS?

One of the most common themes of real estate analysts is that people buy neighborhoods, not just houses. For some time, housing studies have stressed the importance of neighborhood characteristics as a major determinant of housing choice; there is evidence that the neighborhood context directly affects both the decision to move into, and the decision to leave, a particular area. Economists have paid particular attention to those characteristics of transitional neighborhoods that contribute to outmigration.[30] Some survey research, focusing on the causes for householders' dissatisfaction with their housing situation, has suggested that for both low-income and higher-income families neighborhood variables may be more important contributors to dissatisfaction than the physical condition of the housing unit.[31]

Rolf Goetze has argued that urban housing programs cannot succeed if they do not recognize the importance of neighborhood variables as decisive influences on housing choice. Goetze contends that the motivation provided by the neighborhood context is more critical than household income in predicting whether housing will be well maintained. In a neighborhood perceived as "desirable," people are willing to devote very large shares of their income to housing, whereas in "undesirable" neighborhoods even those who could afford to maintain or upgrade their housing will probably not do so. Even massive housing subsidies "seem unable to induce those with a choice to live in the 'wrong' neighborhoods."[32] Not surprisingly, Goetze concludes that the condition of the neighborhood is a crucial determinant of housing values: "Because neighborhood context has a strong influence on the behavior of all the housing actors, it sharply influences market values."[33]

Goetze's conclusion, that the value of an individual property depends heavily on the behavior of all other investors in the neighborhood, is just one example of the strong emphasis that urban analysts place on the investment climate as the key to urban revitalization. Recognizing that the viability of urban communities is directly related to the willingness of mortgage lenders, landlords, and individual homebuyers to invest their capital, researchers and community activists have turned their attention to banks, savings and loans, credit unions, revolving loan funds, and other institutions that mediate the flow of capital into urban housing markets. Redlining, the practice of refusing to lend money for home purchases or repairs in certain neighborhoods classified as too risky, has come under heavy attack by public interest groups across the country.

But if the relationship between housing investments and neighborhood vitality is well established, we know much less about precisely what elements of the residential environment make a "desirable" or "undesirable" location. Surely one important variable is the type of housing, particularly whether the area is dominated by single-family detached housing or multifamily units. Another is the dominant form of tenure—ownership compared with renting. Proximity to employment and retail centers ordinarily counts heavily in an area's appeal to residents, as does the general condition of its housing stock. The composition of a neighborhood's population by income level, race, ethnicity, age, etc., is yet another factor to be considered by residents in choosing a location, although it generally ranks below the physical conditions of home and neighborhoods as a locational factor.[34]

Despite the sizable literature on the factors influencing residential mobility,[35] very little is known about the contribution to residential satisfaction that is made by public investments in community facilities. Do the city's outlays for parks, swimming pools, branch libraries, fire stations, etc., contribute to maintaining neighborhood stability? Conversely, is the absence of this kind of public investment correlated with housing decline? Certainly the findings cited earlier, regarding the importance of the neighborhood context in determining housing preferences and housing values, would suggest that the presence of such amenities could have a significant impact on consumer preferences. Moreover, the attitudes expressed by many practicing planners suggest that they believe this connection exists. For example, a 1975 study by the American Society of Planning Officials examined the development policies of thirteen communities, and found that eleven of the thirteen reported using "location and access to facilities" as a means of controlling growth.[36] A 1977 survey of 105 communities generally confirmed these findings; it showed that fifty-nine percent of the localities surveyed claimed to use the location of public facilities to influence growth.[37] After reviewing these and other available studies, the authors of a wide-ranging literature survey on the subject of capital improvements and development management concluded that "public investment decisions are often based explicitly on the assumed effects of capital improvements," but they acknowledged that "empirical tests of these assumptions are few and far between."[38]

Virtually all of the discussion concerning the impact of public investments on housing markets has focused on growth areas in the suburbs. The goal for planners has been to control new development, sometimes even to discourage new development, by the judicious siting of new roads, utilities, fire stations, and schools. But what about the application of this strategy to central cities? Can we presume that public improvements will increase the attractiveness of already developed neighborhoods, and perhaps even stabilize declining ones? That is certainly the view expressed by the Philadelphia planners who drafted the city's Comprehensive Plan in 1960. Seeing community facilities as an important contributor to the quality of neighborhoods, they hoped to maintain and enhance Philadelphia's residential areas by large investments in such facilities:

> The quality and location of Philadelphia's recreation areas, schools, libraries, health facilities, and governmental services are as important to the city's vitality as its industries, houses, and transportation system.[39]

And it is not only planners who see a connection between capital improvements and neighborhood vitality. Much of the conflict over the city's capital program is based on the popular conception that the construction of a new neighborhood school, library, or pool brings benefits beyond the direct services provided to the users. It represents an investment in the neighborhood as a whole. That is precisely why the discrimination issues raised earlier in this chapter are crucial in any discussion of capital facilities. That is also why the announcement of cutbacks or shutdowns of neighborhood facilities generates such intense opposition. Most residents perceive such an action as contributing to neighborhood decline, whether or not they themselves make use of the facility.

My task in chapter 4 will be to examine this question of the impact of public improvements on neighborhood residential markets. I will compare the pattern of postwar capital spending in Philadelphia with the pattern of neighborhood change, to see what connections exist between the two. At issue is the fundamental question of whether public spending leads and influences private market investments, or simply follows the patterns set by private development.


## THE POLITICS OF THE CAPITAL BUDGETING PROCESS

Conventional wisdom holds that if you want to know what a government's values are, you need only look at its budget to find out. Aaron Wildavsky put the matter as well as anyone when he said:

> If one asks, "Who gets what the government has to give?" then the answers for a moment in time are recorded in the budget. If one looks at politics as a process by which the government mobilizes resources to meet pressing problems, then the budget is a focus of these efforts.[40]

Wildavsky's point is of course that a society's pattern of public spending reflects its values and priorities, and the budget document is the single best description of that spending pattern.

But some of the more recent literature in the field of policy analysis suggests that the budget document alone cannot provide a clear picture of a community's values unless it is accompanied by information about (1) what external forces constrained budgetary choices from the beginning of the process, and (2) what kinds of allocative decisions are delegated to the bureaucrats who implement the budget.

Taking the latter point first—we have seen earlier in this chapter that scholars studying the outcomes of municipal decision making have disagreed about whether city governments systematically discriminate against poor and black neighborhoods. Yet virtually all of them have discovered that city service departments do allocate their resources differentially across neighborhoods, with some getting disproportionately high, and others disproportionately low, levels of service. What determines the differences? Not the budget as a document, since budgets rarely specify which particular client groups or neighborhoods are to be served by various departments. Rather, it is bureaucrats working within programs who make these important allocative decisions using sets of decision rules—regulated procedures for delivering services—which are developed by bureaucratic agencies in order to rationalize their task. These rules, while they have definable distributive consequences, are rarely consistent in favoring one segment of the community over others. One reason for the inconsistency, even within a single agency, is that such decision rules are often established by relatively low-ranking employees. Michael Lipsky[41] and others have shown that the work routines adopted by so-called street level bureaucrats may have significant distributive consequences that are totally unforeseen by the legislative bodies that formulate the budget. The result of the multitude of decisions made daily by city employees is that distributive outcomes are seldom perceived, much less controlled, by high-level city officials. Robert Lineberry has observed that

> there are two remarkable things about decision rules in the bureaucratic allocations of public services. The first is how low in the bureaucratic hierarchy decision rules are formulated and implemented. The second is how insulated the rule-makers are from external constraints.[42]

The implication of Lineberry's observation is that by adopting an annual budget, the city council does not necessarily determine who gets what the government has to give. To a great extent that determination depends upon invisible, low-level bureaucrats who operate the city's programs from week to week.

One of my concerns in this study is the tension between the city council as the budget-making body and the city administration as the implementer of the capital budget. In addressing this issue, it is useful to emphasize that my subject here is *capital* budgets as opposed to *operating* budgets. The process of capital budgeting is a neglected topic in the literature on public finance.[43] Yet capital budgeting must be studied separately from operating budgets because the difference in the nature of these two types of budgets suggests rather different relationships between legislators and bureaucrats. Take, for example, my earlier observation about the well-documented influence of "street-level bureaucrats" in allocating resources by their routine decision rules. Operating budgets and capital budgets differ in the extent to which they specify where, and for what constituencies, the money is to be spent. As we have already remarked, operating budgets rarely dictate just how operating funds will be divided across the city's neighborhoods. In contrast, the vast majority of funds contained in the annual capital budget are targeted at specific project sites, making it reasonably easy to see the geographical distribution of benefits throughout the city. Thus, the capital budget allows minimal discretion to municipal bureaucrats, at least as regards the spatial allocation of the funds, whereas operating budgets offer city departments a wide latitude in deciding where to spend their budgeted moneys.

Moreover, the fact that public works expenditures are made in large amounts, with highly visible results, means that elected politicians maintain a keen interest in the city's capital allocations. Whereas voters may not detect discrepancies in the allocation of police patrols among districts or know whether trash pickup occurs more frequently in some neighborhoods than others, they cannot fail to notice where new schools, libraries, or swimming pools are built. It is not surprising then that much of the political conflict surrounding the capital budget each year is centered on the geographic distribution of funds.

Given these circumstances, we might presume that the legislative branch of city government has both more opportunity and more incentive to control the way in which departments spend capital funds than to control their expenditure of operating moneys. But in fact we shall see that Philadelphia's city council exerts little control over the implementation of its capital budget. Granted, the opening up of city politics to new constituencies in the 1960s and 1970s made the process of budget formulation more visible to the community. Whereas the capital plans of the 1950s were produced by city planners in collaboration with a small civic elite, today's debate on the city's annual capital budget is far more open, and the recommendations made by city planners about which projects to include or exclude are more frequently challenged by city council members and neighborhood activists. And as chapter 5 will show, council members and their constituents have sometimes joined forces to resist cutbacks and closings proposed by facilities planners. Even more significant than the struggles over particular projects, however, are the questions raised by council members and others about the administration's fundamental development priorities, especially as regards the balance between downtown and neighborhood development.

Does the intensified political debate surrounding the annual capital budget mean that the city administration is more accountable to the legislature for carrying out the budget? That optimistic conclusion is not necessarily warranted. If anything, the administration's role has increased as city bureaucrats have taken on the task of selecting from the council's overly optimistic capital programs which projects the city can actually afford to build.

Besides illuminating the respective roles of legislators and bureaucrats in capital budgeting, this case study sheds light on the constraints facing urban policy makers, whether in the legislature or the bureaucracy. This is a topic that has occupied many scholars in the urban politics field in recent years and has spawned a lively debate—a debate whose starting point is the common observation that politicians with widely differing beliefs, backgrounds, and constituencies are increasingly giving highest priority to development programs that support the growth of business in the community.

For example, Pagano and Moore's study of capital spending in American cities shows that from 1957 to 1970 outlays for social overhead capital (i.e., neighborhood facilities) rose at a faster rate than outlays for economic overhead capital (i.e., developmental expenditures). However, in the early 1970s this trend reversed itself, and American cities across the board began to increase EOC expenditures at a faster rate than SOC expenditures.[44] What accounts for this almost universal pattern of policy?

For some scholars the explanation is that business groups tend to have the best political organization in cities. Ever since the earliest commentaries on postwar urban renewal programs, political scientists have emphasized the role played by business representatives, either as individuals or within associations, in shaping the capital programs of American cities. The constellation of business interests most active in promoting urban renewal, including real estate developers, lawyers, bankers, utilities, major retailers, and newspaper editors, has been labeled the "progrowth coalition."[45] What its members have in common is an overriding interest in seeing the urban space used as intensively as possible to promote economic growth. They see the city as a "growth machine."

This notion of a vigorous progrowth coalition working to influence local development efforts is plausible to anyone who has observed the level of public support furnished by elite business organizations for various cities' proposals to build convention centers,[46] sports complexes,[47] and other major public investments designed to bring business to town. Typically, such business groups are in the forefront of major downtown initiatives, but demonstrate far less enthusiasm for neighborhood renewal schemes. It is perhaps natural to conclude that it is their ability to dominate in local political struggles that has led to the imbalance between downtown and neighborhood priorities that so many community groups complain about.

Yet some scholars have questioned whether the probusiness outcomes observed so frequently in urban politics are really the result of direct pressure from the business community. Indeed, some city governments appear to cater to the preferences of businesses even when they do not participate at all in local politics. Still, their interests normally prevail because cities depend on them for economic survival. If large real estate developers or industrialists decide to move elsewhere, their actions will undermine the local tax base. Hence, in order to keep them satisfied, local governments serve their needs, even when business representatives are not personally active in politics.[48] This suggests that there are economic structures operating in cities that produce probusiness policies, quite apart from the political activism of business men and women.

The case for "economic structuralism," as it is sometimes called,[49] is best presented in Paul Peterson's *City Limits*. Peterson argues that the pressure to compete within the national economy exerts far more influence over urban public policy than the cities' internal political struggles:

> The place of the city within the larger political economy of the nation fundamentally affects the policy choices that cities make. In making these decisions, cities select those policies which are in the interests of the city, taken as a whole. It is these city interests, not the internal struggles for power within cities, that limit city policies and condition what local governments do.[50]

The result of this external pressure is that local policy makers tend to favor what Peterson calls "developmental" policies and to avoid "redistributive" policies. Developmental policies contribute to the city's economic well-being, either by protecting the community's fiscal resources or by promoting growth and expansion. They may do so either directly, as when the city offers free land and tax concessions to an incoming manufacturer, or indirectly, as when the city extends its transportation system or reforms its tax structure in an effort to improve its attractiveness as a locale for economic activity. Developmental policies are essential to sustaining a city's market position. That is why city officials so consistently favor them over community programs, especially those in low-income communities. In contrast, redistributive policies, which tax the resources of some citizens to benefit others, are seldom pursued vigorously by policymakers. Cities simply cannot afford to undertake redistributive programs in poor neighborhoods, for fear of weakening their market position.

In some ways this case study of capital spending in Philadelphia confirms the theories of the economic structuralists, yet at the same time it raises some questions about their model. As Peterson and other proponents of structuralism would have predicted, the capital budgeting process *has* increasingly favored developmental priorities, as the city's competition with other metropolitan areas has intensified. Yet my findings challenge Peterson's notion that under these circumstances, redistribution is impossible. The expenditure data on community facilities show a clearly redistributive tendency that actually increased over the thirty-year period from 1950 to 1980.

Nor can I conclude, as do the adherents of the growth machine model, that Philadelphia's capital budget is the captive of a progrowth coalition that makes decisions about when and where to build. Admittedly, the decade immediately following World War II was one of extraordinary business participation in city planning. As clearly as any other American city, Philadelphia in the 1950s was run by a business/government partnership that determined the direction of urban renewal. But as we will see, the strength of that business/government alliance diminished dramatically in the 1960s and 1970s. And yet, even during periods when Philadelphia business elites were alienated from city government, the emphasis in the capital budget remained on projects favorable to their interests.

The importance of this case study lies, then, not in its ability to confirm either of these important explanatory frameworks in its entirety. Its contribution is in pointing to the importance of a variable that is often overlooked by both analytical approaches—namely, the structure of the capital markets on which the city depends to finance its construction programs. For a large share of its investment dollars, the city turns to the same pools of capital and the same financial institutions as any other borrower. And cities must play according to the rules established by those who control the capital markets. As we shall see in chapter 6, urban investment decisions are strongly influenced by the conditions under which that investment capital is made available.

One criticism leveled at economic structuralism is that by placing all of its explanatory emphasis on structural variables, it virtually excludes any consideration of partisan or community politics as a determinant of policies. Let me reassure the reader that local political struggles are not to be overlooked in this account of Philadelphia's capital budgeting. Chapter 5 discusses the increasingly strident conflicts that have taken place within the city council's chambers over questions of where and how the city invests its own tax dollars. Yet the conclusion that must be drawn from the expenditure data is that over time, these skirmishes have less and less impact. For the decisions have shifted more and more into the administrative arena. And the emphasis in construction has shifted gradually away from projects that must be supported with local tax revenues, toward projects that can be financed in other ways. Chapter 6 will suggest that these shifts have had the unfortunate effect of weakening the government's accountability to taxpayers and voters.

The issue of public accountability, it must be said, is more complex in the case of capital investments than it is for other policy areas. What makes this set of decisions different from most others confronted by local government is that their consequences extend so far into the future. Not only do future residents inherit the physical results of today's capital decisions, in the form of roads, buildings, and parks; they also inherit the responsibility of paying for them, since the financing mechanisms usually spread the cost of these projects over their useful life. If today's tight budgets lead city officials to cut back on maintenance and new construction, then future generations of Philadelphians will inherit an inadequate physical plant. At the other extreme, a policy of reckless capital spending by today's politicians could transfer an intolerable financial burden to future taxpayers. Thus, capital planning involves balancing the interests of today's residents, businesses, neighborhoods, and institutions with those of the next generation.

# 2

# Philadelphia as a Case Study

W HY choose Philadelphia for a study of capital planning? One reason is that city planning has unusually deep roots in this city. From its seventeenth-century origins, Philadelphia was distinguished among North American settlements by the degree to which land-use planning influenced its shape and structure. The ground plan for William Penn's initial settlement in 1682 borrowed its key features from a well-known proposal for the rebuilding of London after the Great Fire of 1666: a central town square placed at the intersection of the two main streets, surrounded by four lesser squares acting as focal points for each of the four quadrants of the settlement. While not the only early American community to be built on a plan, Penn's Philadelphia was surely the largest and most ambitious in scope. In commenting upon this distinction, one historical survey of Philadelphia architecture suggested the long-term influence on the city that stemmed from these orderly beginnings:

> More than any other community on the eastern seaboard it was a reflection of the ideals of the Age of Reason. Even with the further compromises that were to follow, Philadelphia's sense of order and established matrix of growth contrasted significantly with other communities' random collection of narrow, angled streets haphazardly placed.[1]

A more immediate justification for choosing Philadelphia as our case study is the reputation the city earned as a national leader in planning and redevelopment in the decades following World War II. During the 1950s and 1960s, Philadelphia was featured regularly at national meetings of architects, planners, and redevelopment officials as a model for other cities to emulate. *Time, Life,* and other national magazines carried colorful accounts of the massive renewal and rebuilding that was being guided in Philadelphia by a coalition of enlightened politicians, dedicated civic leaders, and skilled planners. The international reputation of Edmund Bacon, the architect who directed the Philadelphia City Planning Commission from 1949 to 1970, drew a cadre of energetic and qualified young planners to the city, making it a center whose influence extended over the entire planning profession. What most distinguished Philadelphia's postwar renewal program was the city's ability to move reasonably quickly from paper to bricks-and-mortar—to take the architectural visions of Bacon and others, and to generate the financial backing, the political acceptance, and the administrative and logistical support to get them built. The key to this process was capital programming. The authors of a detailed study of the city's capital planning process in the 1950s were understating the case in asserting that "Philadelphia has carried capital programming as far as—some would say farther than—any other major American jurisdiction."[2] Jeanne Lowe's 1967 survey of redevelopment activities in cities across the country offers this glowing assessment of Philadelphia's achievements: "Of all the big cities, Philadelphia has come closest to a comprehensive approach to the complex of challenges confronting our urban centers. . . . Perhaps more than any other big city, Philadelphia has had to rely on informed long-range plans, design excellence, aggressive action strategies for its survival."[3]


## PLANNING AND REFORM POLITICS

It is impossible to understand the city's postwar development programs without recognizing the strong links between the city's physical rebuilding and its political rebirth. The emergence of an effective planning apparatus coincided with the advent of reform government; both reflected a repudiation of machine politics in favor of rational, enlightened planning. After decades of control by an increasingly corrupt Republican machine, the city's business and civic elites coalesced in the late 1940s to push for a new city charter that would enhance the power of the mayor, place the responsibility for managing the city's main operating departments in the hands of a professional managing director, strengthen the civil service system, and carefully circumscribe the powers of the reorganized city council. Only seven months after the new Home Rule Charter was passed in a special election in April 1951, reform Mayor Joseph Clark swept into office, bringing on his coattails fifteen reform Democrats as members of the reorganized city council. Their victory "unleashed powerful sentiments for renovation of the city's politics and orientation toward public responsibilities."[4]

Chief among the public responsibilities assumed by the new reform administration was that of physical redevelopment of the aging industrial center. Civic rejuvenation was identified with urban renewal in the central business district to create new office and commercial space, and with development of new residential areas, especially on the open land of the northeastern, northwestern, and southwestern sections of Philadelphia. The decade of the 1930s had witnessed little building activity in the city, some suburban migration, and generally declining real estate values. In the early 1940s, the war had further limited housing production. Consequently, pent-up demand was intense in the late 1940s and early 1950s.

So closely intertwined were the movements toward physical and political regeneration in postwar Philadelphia that in a 1957 address to the American Institute of Planners, Richardson Dilworth, the reform Democrat who succeeded Joseph Clark as Mayor, observed: "When you think about it, our reform movement really was sparkplugged by the planners and not the politicians!" The most detailed historical account of Philadelphia's reform period, authored by one of the participants, confirms Dilworth's view, suggesting in fact that the reformers' interest in city planning actually preceded their interest in governmental reform.[5]

This is perhaps not surprising, given the fact that housing had provided the focal point for earlier reform activities in the city. The great contribution of the housing reformers was to recognize that slum conditions were not solely attributable to idleness and drunkenness on the part of their inhabitants—a typical nineteenth-century view of the causes of blight and squalor. As early as 1895, reformers persuaded the state legislature to pass a bill that established laws regarding fireproofing, light, and ventilation for all tenements of more than four stories. In 1904 a group of them known as the Octavia Hill Association published a study titled *Housing Conditions in Philadelphia*. In words and photographs, it documented the unsafe and unsanitary conditions in which many of the city's poor people lived, and became the basis of a successful campaign to lobby the state legislature for a better tenement inspection bill. Building upon this early accomplishment, housing reformers in sixty different organizations cooperated to establish in 1909 the Philadelphia Housing Association, whose efforts included lobbying for passage and enforcement of the first municipal housing code in 1915, the first Philadelphia zoning ordinance in 1933, and national-level housing legislation in the 1930s and 1940s.

It was therefore natural that housing and city planning issues should be the starting point for the concerned business executives, lawyers, bankers, academics, and other civic leaders who began meeting as early as 1940 to discuss the future of their city. Operating in several incarnations under different labels (the City Policy Committee, the Joint Committee on City Planning, the Citizens' Council on City Planning), this core group of citizen activists monitored the public improvement projects proposed by city government and offered criticisms and evaluations. Although a 1942 ordinance had established official planning machinery within the municipal government, the influence of these energetic outsiders was substantial. "In fact the [city] council refused to take any action on the capital program until it had carefully studied the recommendations of the Citizens' Council."[6]

To no one's surprise, the issue of physical planning figured prominently in the 1951 charter revision, which made important changes in the City Planning Commission that had been established in the early 1940s. The 1951 charter, still in effect in Philadelphia today, assigned to the nine-member commission a quasi-independent status, outside the realm of direct mayoral control and yet strongly influenced by the members of the mayor's cabinet who participated as ex officio members of the commission (the managing director, the director of finance, and the city representative). The Commission's role in preparing the annual capital budget was described by the charter in detail, including the annual timetable by which the capital budget was to be transmitted from the commission to the mayor and then to city council. Moreover, the document charged the Planning Commission with preparing each year a *six*-year capital program to accompany the *one*-year capital budget, in order to show how the short-term spending projected for the coming year would fit into longer-term plans. Yet another of the Planning Commission's obligations set forth in the 1951 charter was its responsibility to develop a comprehensive plan for the city showing present and planned physical development. Once adopted, the Physical Development Plan was clearly intended to guide the city government's future development decisions:

> No public way, ground or open space, or building or structure paid for in whole or in part with funds from the City Treasury, or a public utility for which a franchise is necessary from the City, shall be developed, improved, or constructed *unless recommendations of the City Planning Commission as to location and size pursuant to the Physical Development Plan shall have been first requested and obtained.*[7] [emphasis added].

It took longer than expected to produce this plan, but finally in May 1960 the Planning Commission fulfilled its statutory obligation by transmitting to the mayor and council a twenty-year Comprehensive Plan that the commission labeled "a blueprint for the Philadelphia of tomorrow."

Even from this brief summary of the 1951 charter reform, it must be obvious that the reformers' goal with respect to city planning as well as to other aspects of city policy was to minimize the influence of partisan politics on the postwar reconstruction of Philadelphia. The reformers' platform reads like the standard Progressive litany: they aspired to purge municipal government of corruption, install a new professionalism in city departments, improve the efficiency of services, and minimize the influence of patronage in filling city jobs. Rather than using public improvements like fire stations and recreation centers simply to lubricate the political machine, the reformers hoped to apply a combination of enlightened politics and professional expertise to decide when and where they should be built. To the dismay of many old-time regulars in the Philadelphia Democratic party, the good-government forces backing the reform administrations of the 1950s expected public, not partisan, considerations to prevail in constructing community facilities, formulating zoning ordinances, issuing building permits, assessing properties on the tax rolls, and exercising the city's power of eminent domain.

## EARLY EMPHASIS ON PHYSICAL REDEVELOPMENT

In other respects as well, the record of Philadelphia's reform era reflects the influence of the earlier Progressive movement, which was historically linked to the emergence of city planning across the United States. In Philadelphia as elsewhere, the City Beautiful movement was first manifested in monumental civic projects whose physical appearance was as important as their function. In 1905 a citizens' committee persuaded the city council to construct a broad tree-lined boulevard connecting City Hall with the new art museum at the edge of the city's sprawling Fairmount Park, thus signaling the start of city planning in Philadelphia. By 1909 the City Parks Association was campaigning for a "Comprehensive City Plan."

Like their early twentieth-century counterparts, Philadelphia reformers of the 1950s identified civic betterment with physical renewal and beautification. There is no better illustration of the visual and physical orientation of the reform movement than the celebrated Better Philadelphia Exhibition of 1947. In an attempt to excite widespread support for a major renewal effort, the Chamber of Commerce and the blue-ribbon Citizens' Council on City Planning joined forces shortly after World War II ended, to raise money for an unprecedented local exhibition that would get the public to think in concrete terms about the city's future. It is indicative of the way the reformers operated that the project was conceived and carried to fruition by a coalition of civic leaders working with the staff of the City Planning Commission. Elected politicians, including the mayor, had only a tangential connection to the exhibition until opening day, when a good number of them attended in order to be counted among Philadelphia's forward-looking thinkers. The exhibit portrayed in meticulous detail a host of projects that would change the face of the city over the next thirty years, yet virtually none of them had received any official endorsement from the city council or even from the planning commission as a body. They had leapt from the imaginations of architects Oskar Stonorov and Louis Kahn and a younger planner named Edmund Bacon.

The massive display included dioramas of different sections of the city in different historical periods, one of which was the "time-space machine," a masterpiece of visual drama depicting the city's growth from 1782 to 1947. Once the entire map was lit up to show Philadelphia in 1947, a pendulum swung over it, spreading a dark shadow (blight) across the city's decaying areas. A large sculpted hand pointed out at the audience with the words, "It's up to you!"

Another example of the exhibit's showmanship was its fourteen-by-thirty-foot centerpiece, a motorized scale model of the central business district, whose component sections flipped over to reveal the gleaming new structures and streets that were proposed to replace the worn-out city center. The organizers managed to persuade Gimbel's Department Store to provide space for the exhibit, on the theory that such a location would maximize its public exposure. It was meant to excite people about the possibilities inherent in city planning, and it drew an average of sixty-five hundred people a day.[8]

Commenting thirty years later on the conception of city planning that prevailed in Philadelphia in the 1940s, Robert Mitchell, Director of the City Planning Commission from 1943 to 1948 and a key organizer of the 1947 exhibition, mused:

> I should say that in those days the concepts of city planning were largely having to do with the physical construction of the city and were not concerned with the social and economic development to the extent that is the case today in planning in most cities.[9]

If anything, the narrowly physical orientation toward planning acknowledged by Mitchell was reinforced by his successor, Edmund Bacon, of whom Kirk Petshek wrote in his chronicle of the reform era:

> The staff assembled by Bacon was, in line with his own predilections, especially strong in physical design. . . . Despite public lip service to the importance of the social and economic factors in development, Bacon never modified his personal priority, which was design.[10]

Many accounts written in the 1970s and 1980s about the reformers of the 1950s have been critical of them because of their alleged tendency to separate the physical from the socioeconomic aspects of development, focusing their attention on the former while neglecting the latter. As the quotation from Mitchell demonstrates, even some participants in the reform movement have accepted this interpretation. But the motives of reformers, I think, should be read somewhat differently. In emphasizing the physical dimensions of renewal, many of those involved in the reform movement believed they were directly addressing the city's social and economic problems. Far from separating the two aspects of development, they, like the earlier Progressives, saw the solution of social and economic problems as dependent upon physical reconstruction. To a significant extent, they subscribed to the "positive environmentalism" that Paul Boyer has shown to be central to the Progressive ideology.

What is positive environmentalism? It is the view expressed by the General Federation of Women's Clubs in 1909 that "bad physical environment means bad moral environment,"[11] and thus contributes to idleness, drunkenness, prostitution, family breakdown, and even violence. According to this view, slums were literally the cause of many social ills. Tenement investigators in Cleveland warned that "the physical conditions under which these people live lessen their power to resist evil," and Jane Addams was even more specific in charging that tenement life was a main contributor to prostitution because the lack of privacy broke down young girls' natural modesty and reserve.[12] Given such premises, it is easy to see why the Progressives assigned the very highest priority to physical rebuilding of the urban environment. Tenement reform groups were active in many big cities including the city of Philadelphia, where the Octavia Hill Association and later the Philadelphia Housing Association pressed for more regulation of tenement landlords.

At roughly the same time and for similar reasons, the municipal recreation movement emerged. Settlement houses provided one approach to the problem of supervising the leisure time of urban youngsters in order to protect them from the wicked influences of the street and slum. Another approach was the campaign of park advocates for municipal playgrounds and neighborhood parks that would be staffed and equipped to provide both supervised and unsupervised recreation activities. (One lasting legacy of this period is the minimum space and facilities standards for urban populations devised in the early twentieth century, some of which still guide decision makers in urban recreation departments.) Other Progressives stressed the value of providing some parks with only natural landscaping and few facilities, as quiet retreats from congested city life. Henry Ward Beecher is reported to have remarked approvingly about Brooklyn's Prospect Park, that its "divine element of beauty in nature" would inspire the poor to "gentle thought and grateful silence."[13]

Beecher's observation hints at the element of social control inherent in the Progressives' "positive environmentalism." The reformers promoted better housing, more parks, and other environmental improvements not only to bring greater comfort and safety to the lives of the wretched urban poor, but also to shape their attitudes and behavior in ways that would strengthen the urban moral order and guarantee civil peace. In the words of a Boston law professor writing in 1912,

An important result of these city movements is the development of civic interest and pride on the part of the people. A city which does nothing except to police and clean the streets means little. But, when it adds schools, libraries, galleries, parks, baths, lights, heat, homes, and transportation, it awakens interest in itself. The citizen cares for the city which shows some care for him . . . and he becomes a good citizen because it is his city.[14]

The idea that physical redevelopment could contribute to solving social and economic problems remained alive in Philadelphia in the 1940s and 1950s, as it did in cities across the country. The postwar emphasis on clearing slums and replacing them with public housing testifies to its survival. Housing professionals at the national level pressed Congress for increased funds for municipal building programs on the grounds that America

> must achieve for every family a home where children can be reared in decency and health, where they may develop the mental- moral vigor and pride in community that will make them first class citizens.[15]

And Congress responded with the 1949 Housing Act.

Granted, there were other reasons as well for local officials to favor physical redevelopment as an approach to social problems. The first and most obvious explanation for this is simply that city governments have few means of directly influencing family incomes. Many important causes of family poverty are rooted in regional or national economic trends over which cities have little control. Unemployment, for example, may strike an urban family because of shifts in the national (or even international) demand for a product, or because an employer decides to move his operation to another region or another country. City governments have very limited ability to influence such shifts. Nor can municipalities regulate levels of migration into the cities of unskilled poor from other regions and other countries.

Second, it would mean political and financial suicide for city governments to undertake large-scale income distribution programs on their own. Taxing the incomes of the "haves" to pay income support to the "have nots" would surely accelerate the exodus of middle-class urban dwellers. Our governmental system acknowledges this reality, by locating our large-scale income transfer programs at the state and federal levels. Social Security, Aid to Families with Dependent Children, Medicaid and Medicare are America's major income-transfer programs; all are subsidized predominantly by federal taxes or by a combination of state and federal funds.

Third and most important, the tax structure of most American cities offers a strong incentive for local officials to see blight as the most important manifestation of poverty. Local revenues in most cities are collected from property taxes. When neighborhoods deteriorate physically, property values decline and city revenues suffer. Thus, city governments lose money when they lose sections of the city to creeping vandalism and decay.

But having noted these practical considerations, we must also recognize the influence exerted, at both the national and local levels, by postwar reformers who saw physical redevelopment as a way to address social problems. Discussing postwar housing policy in Philadelphia, Conrad Weiler has labeled the strategy which prevailed until the late 1950s the "physical-structure approach," noting the influence on city policy of Pennsylvania's 1937 housing statute that flatly asserted that substandard housing conditions "subject the moral standards of the people to bad influences which have permanent deleterious social effects," and "increase the violation of the criminal laws."[16] Mayor Clark himself was known to believe that "growing blight was related to poor health, crime, and other social problems."[17]

## THE 1960 COMPREHENSIVE PLAN

Not surprisingly, given the reformers' assumption that the city's physical decay was directly related to its social problems, they chose to focus the 1960 Comprehensive Plan for Philadelphia on the city's physical condition. One analysis of that 1960 document published twenty years later decried its "physical design bias," observing that

> The Plan was devised as a physical development plan, interpreting "physical" in a narrow sense. Expressways, parks, health facilities, clearance of industrial land and residential density were the Plan's primary topics, not unemployment, racial discrimination or poverty.[18]

As one of the first American cities to organize a large-scale urban renewal program in response to federal subsidies, Philadelphia had initially adopted a policy of concentrating its effort on the most blighted areas of the city. Several of its most dilapidated neighborhoods were targeted for earliest attention, with those structures that were either beyond repair or too expensive to repair being demolished, and those that were salvageable being rebuilt. Looking back on this "worst- first" strategy of the 1950s, William Rafsky, the city's development coordinator in that period, explained that "we thought in that way we would get rid of this cancer in the city."[19] Rafsky's use of the medical metaphor illustrates the prevailing view that physical blight was in effect a "carrier" of social diseases that were spreading through the city's declining neighborhoods.

The same philosophy may account for the favorable treatment accorded to the city's most blighted areas in the 1960 Comprehensive Plan, despite the fact that those areas had little or no representation in the planning process. None of the historical accounts of the politics of the 1960 Comprehensive Plan, even those written by participants, disputes the elitist nature of that process. From its inception in the early twentieth century, city planning in Philadelphia had been carried on by a series of commissions on which the particular faces changed, but the representation of interests remained unchanged. Sam Bass Warner's description of the situation in the 1920s fits the 1940s and 1950s almost as well:

> The people who planned, or who sat on planning commissions, were downtown merchants, utility, transit, and bank directors, real estate men, railroad and ocean transport carriers, and a few professionals (i.e. perennial Philadelphia board sitters, architects, and civil engineers.)[20]

The formal vehicle for citizen input into the postwar planning process was the Citizens' Council on City Planning (CCCP), a blue-ribbon civic group composed of the same interests identified by Warner as being influential in the 1920s, the only difference being that lawyers, architects, academics, and other professionals played a more prominent role in the postwar era than they had earlier. (For example, in the early 1950s the CCCP's executive committee was composed of three attorneys, a landscape architect, and an investment banker.) As a watchdog organization, the Citizens' Council conducted a detailed evaluation of each year's capital budget in the 1950s and 1960s, not only recommending projects for addition or deletion, but also ranking the various projects according to their importance and urgency. The CCCP was also formally integrated into the preparation of the 1960 Comprehensive Plan, establishing for that purpose a series of subcommittees which paralleled the main components of the plan (there was, for example, one subcommittee for community facilities, one for transportation, one for residential planning, etc.). The work of these subcommittees in reviewing every aspect of the plan was ultimately circulated in a published report, and the correspondence that flowed between the Planning Commission, city offices, and the CCCP during the plan's preparation suggests that the influence of the citizen activists was substantial.[21]

What kinds of priorities were reflected in a document that was produced by this coalition of planning professionals and civic elites? If we look first at the section on community facilities, we find surprisingly generous provisions made for the inner city. A good illustration of this pattern is the plan's allocation of new playgrounds and playfields across the city. Figure 2.1 shows the city of Philadelphia divided into its main subsections, and the accompanying table (table 2.1) provides information about the playgrounds and playfields allocated to each of those subsections by the 1960 Plan. The table shows that the plan assigned the largest numbers of new facilities to three inner city districts (South Philadelphia, West Philadelphia, and Lower North Philadelphia) and one district lying outside the inner city (Near Northeast). The fourth and fifth columns of the table show that the three inner city sections slated for the most new facilities were also the sections with the lowest median incomes and the highest proportions of nonwhite residents in the city. Moreover, as the third column suggests, none of the three was expected by planners to gain significantly in population by 1980. Of them, West Philadelphia was the section most clearly in need of investment, since it had substantially fewer acres in playgrounds and playfields in 1960 than any other part of the city, and since its population was expected to remain relatively stable. (Column 3 shows that planners expected only a five percent increase in population.) But the justification on numerical grounds is more difficult to make for South Philadelphia and Lower North Philadelphia, both of which were expected to sustain heavy population losses by 1980.

The explanation for this somewhat surprising emphasis on new recreation space in declining inner city areas appears to be that planners located recreation improvements not only where they saw the most urgent need for more recreation services, but also where they saw an opportunity to upgrade the physical environment. The plan

**Figure 2.1**
**Planning Analysis Sections**

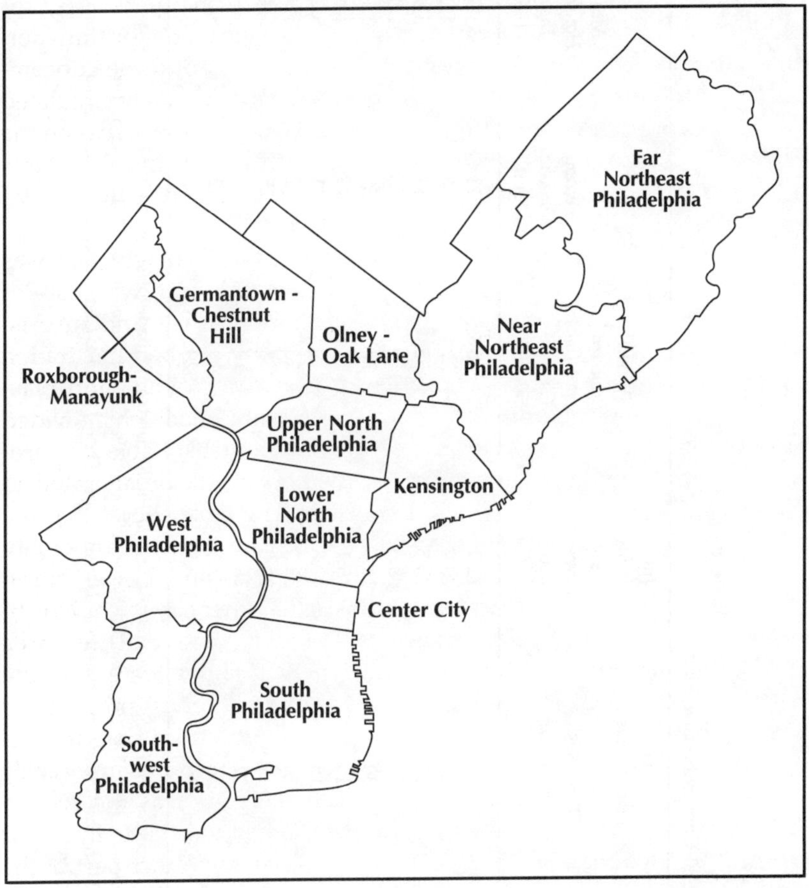

made clear the city's intent "to reduce densities in a large part of the inner areas of the city,"[22] in order to eliminate crowding and to distribute the population in a more rational pattern. After selectively clearing the most dilapidated housing in older neighborhoods, planners had to identify alternative uses for the land that would enhance the environment for the remaining residents. Recreation was an attractive alternative:

Execution of the Recreation Plan will require removal of 435 acres

**Table 2.1**

Playgrounds and Playfields in the 1960 Comprehensive Plan

| | New Playgrounds and Playfields Proposed in 1960 Plan[1] | Playgrounds Existing in 1960 (Acres/ 10,000 Population) | Percent Projected Population Change 1950–1980[2] | Percent Nonwhite 1960[3] | Median Household Income 1960[3] |
|---|---|---|---|---|---|
| Center City | 4 | 12.1 | + 45% | 21% | $3,326 |
| South Philadelphia | 28 | 20.2 | − 27 | 26 | 4,295 |
| Southwest Philadelphia | 17 | 28.5 | + 55 | 11 | 5,495 |
| West Philadelphia | 39 | 8.6 | + 5 | 53 | 4,067 |
| Lower North Philadelphia | 30 | 14.3 | − 28 | 69 | 3,148 |
| Upper North Philadelphia | 16 | 15.1 | − 12 | 19 | 4,687 |
| Kensington | 15 | 49.8 | − 2 | 1 | 5,288 |
| Roxborough-Manayunk | 9 | 33.5 | + 76 | 2 | 5,991 |
| Germantown-Chestnut Hill | 16 | 24.0 | + 58 | 25 | 5,439 |
| Olney-Oak Lane | 22 | 38.7 | + 19 | 4 | 6,014 |
| Near Northeast Philadelphia | 36 | 57.0 | + 19 | 2 | 6,333 |
| Far Northeast Philadelphia | 16 | 150.5 | +529 | 3 | 6,827 |

*Sources:* [1]City Planning Commission, *Inventory of Public Recreation Areas and Public Schools*, Philadelphia, April 1961.
[2]City Planning Commission, *Comprehensive Plan: The Physical Development Plan for the City of Philadelphia*, Philadelphia, 1960.
[3]City Planning Commission, *Recent Historical Trends in Population, Housing, and Socio-Economic Characteristics of Philadelphia Planning Analysis Sections*, Philadelphia, December 1966.

from residential use. This is the most important single step in raising the quality of the residential environment.[23]

Once we understand that planners saw recreation facilities not simply as a service to be dispensed in response to need, but as a tool for enhancing the physical environment, then it is clear why the inner city received such favorable treatment.

## SOCIAL OVERHEAD CAPITAL VERSUS ECONOMIC OVERHEAD CAPITAL

Community facilities, however, represented only one part of the Comprehensive Plan. When looking at the priorities expressed by planners in the 1960 document, we cannot ignore the weight they assigned to economic infrastructure. In fact, the plan allocated fully sixty-five percent of the total twenty-year investment to the development of industrial, commercial and transportation facilities, while the remaining thirty-five percent was expected to go for investments in housing and service facilities. Despite the two-to-one ratio of economic infrastructure investments to housing and service investments, the plan must be seen as unusually generous in its treatment of services to citizens.

For one thing, the transportation category of expenditures enjoyed an artificial advantage simply because the cost of expressways and many other motorways in the plan could be covered almost entirely by federal funds, whereas the outlays for police and fire stations, recreation facilities, libraries, and health centers would have to be raised locally. In that sense, community facilities were more costly items to include in the plan.

Furthermore, in the ten years leading up to publication of the plan, the city had shown a marked preference for spending the bulk of its resources on economic development projects rather than on community facilities. Writing in 1960, after he had left Philadelphia to take a seat in the United States Senate, reform Mayor Joseph Clark attributed the dearth of public investment in such facilities during the 1950s to a general disenchantment with the role of government during the Eisenhower years:

> Much of what has to be done by way of providing new facilities and open areas for the cities falls in the public sector . . . because

there is no immediate profit in the task for the entrepreneur. Community facilities thus become the responsibility of government, and government has been unpopular during the last eight years. So schools, libraries, recreation centers, sewage disposal plants, off-street garages and so on, which belong to the public sector of the economy, have been starved during most of the Fifties.[24]

Other commentators on Philadelphia's capital program in the 1950s have credited Mayor Clark with a positive stance on spending for health, welfare, recreation, and housing, but observed that his successor in 1956, Mayor Richardson Dilworth, did not share this predisposition and shifted priorities away from community facilities and toward economic infrastructure, especially transportation.[25]

It would be a mistake, however, to see this issue as a problem of the postwar period alone. The shortage of funding for community facilities is a perennial problem. The same disposition on the part of the city's leadership can be traced back to the early twentieth century, when even the public schools—a municipal service that was widely supported by the city's business and civic establishment—had trouble securing money to build enough classrooms for the burgeoning school population. According to Warner, "the level of recreation, police, and health services of Philadelphia in the twenties was so low that the entire city could have benefited from more allocations in these directions."[26] But the neighborhoods did not get these investments because the municipal government was too heavily committed to downtown development to have much money left over for community services. Much the same observation could be made about the mid-nineteenth century, when municipal services were shortchanged in favor of municipal investments in canals and railroads that would draw more commerce into the city. In light of this long-standing bias toward economic development projects in the city's public works program, it is really remarkable how *much* of the total investment foreseen in the 1960 Plan was allocated to housing and services.

Their favored standing, however, began to erode almost immediately upon adoption of the plan, as the city administration turned its attention to implementation. The difficulty was that although the 1960 Plan had provided twenty-year goals for capital spending with respect to each of the municipal departments, it had not indicated what the priorities would be among those various goals. Should the total expenditures projected for each department simply be divided by twenty to determine the annual allocations for each department in the capital budget? In that case, the building programs of all the departments would move toward completion at the same steady rate. Or should the city attack its transportation problems first, moving ahead to complete a large share of its total twenty-year program in this field, while postponing other types of projects until later in the twenty-year cycle?

The city administration's approach to deciding such questions reveals again the role of business and professional elites in Philadelphia's postwar planning. The task was assigned to City Economist Kirk Petshek, who devised a scheme that entirely bypassed municipal officials and sought instead the views of civic leaders on the question of which parts of the Comprehensive Plan deserved highest priority. Petshek selected forty leading Philadelphians, including three college presidents, four other academics, three clergymen, two labor leaders, seventeen presidents or executive directors of civic and other nonprofit organizations, and six presidents of banks or other economic enterprises; he asked each of them as individuals to assess the relative long-run importance of all the capital projects contained in plan. Even the City Planning Commission was excluded from this exercise—an omission that its director Edmund Bacon protested. Petshek's response to the Bacon protest offered no apologies for seeking the subjective judgments of a narrow elite circle:

> Our office had not intended to poll different segments of the population by asking the opinion of their official representatives. The idea was rather to get the consolidated opinion of a group of those who are generally regarded as community leaders. . . . If the Planning Commission, as your memo indicates, relies on established channels and the official relations with civic organizations, it will receive only the agreed official stands those organizations are willing to take publicly; thus what would still be missing is the spontaneous expression of individual preferences by those persons who strongly influence civic opinion, privately and confidentially expressed.[27]

What was the outcome of this straightforward exercise in elite consultation? There were six categories of expenditures that the respondents believed should receive priority in the sense that investment should proceed more rapidly in these than in other spending categories. Four of these six preferred categories involved the city's economic infrastructure (industrial renewal, industrial land development, expressways, and the port); one involved neighborhood improvement (residential renewal); and the sixth (mass transit) could arguably be classified as either a service to the citizenry or an economic asset. Among the low-priority categories—that is, those that respondents felt should be completed at a slower rate than the overall plan—we find virtually all other facilities assigned to serve citizens in neighborhoods, with the exceptions of street paving and recreation. The respondents gave lowest priority to expenditures for parks, libraries, traffic control and street lighting, storm flood relief, fire and police stations, while concluding that only street paving and recreation improvements should be pursued at an even rate throughout the twenty-year life of the plan.[28] Whether or not the bias expressed by these respondents in favor of economic infrastructure actually influenced subsequent capital programs may be debated, but the city economist who conducted the survey and presented the results to the mayor's cabinet in 1961 believed it did influence decisions made by the city administration.[29] In any case, we will see in later chapters that the tension between those who emphasize community facilities and those who advocate other types of capital projects continues right down to the most recent capital budgets.

One of the features of the Philadelphia scene that was particularly envied by planning professionals across the country in the 1950s and early 1960s was the legal and political standing accorded to physical planning in the city. Under the 1951 city charter, both the annual capital budgets and the six-year capital programs developed each year by planners needed to be adopted by the city council as ordinances, the capital budget having the status of an appropriation bill. This arrangement gave Philadelphia's capital budget "a status virtually unique among American municipalities."[30] Edmund Bacon once boasted to an audience of planners that the Philadelphia City Council's obligation to adopt a full six-year program by ordinance "lifted the whole matter of recommended community priorities out of the realm of planners aspiring to hopefulness, into that of a political act."[31] As the director of the City Planning Commission for over twenty years, Bacon relished the political dimension of his task. He observed in the mid-1970s after he had left the commission that

> all over the United States there are governments that put out documents that look almost identical to ours visually, but I think almost none of them has gone the step of making it a real political

document. . . . I think we're still the only city, as far as I know, where the capital program is so deeply enmeshed in the realities of the political process.[32]

Similarly, the city charter gave extraordinary legal standing to the 1960 Comprehensive Plan which, once developed, was to be the standard by which all future development proposals were to be judged. Yet neither the Comprehensive Plan nor the six-year capital programs, nor even the annual capital budgets, have been the controlling blueprints that they were intended to be.

Philadelphia's experience with the 1960 Comprehensive Plan raises questions about whether it is in fact desirable for a single planning document, no matter how expertly prepared, to define future development. The most obvious departures from the plan involved the urban highway network that was proposed to speed traffic flows in the city. Two major new arteries, the North Penn Expressway and the Main Line Expressway, were to bring traffic from the northern and western suburbs into midtown, where they would join a new Midtown Loop that could carry traffic across town at high speeds. None of these proposed expressways was ever built, and yet to many observers the failure to implement these grand plans actually proved beneficial to the city in the long run. As one recent study of Philadelphia transportation put it:

> Construction of badly needed facilities was delayed; but in some ways this sluggishness later proved to have had some very beneficial results: it prevented construction of excessively large freeways which would have negatively affected the entire character of Philadelphia.[33]

In contrast to the many departures from the transportation component of the plan, city departments adhered rather closely to the plan's prescriptions for new community facilities. Almost all of the branch libraries projected in the plan were in place by 1980, as were over half of the proposed parks and playgrounds. In fact, the section of the 1960 Plan dealing with recreation and community facilities was by far the most successful in realizing its goal. Here too, however, one might question whether strict adherence to the plan, even if it had been achieved, would have been a desirable course of action. For the planners' recommendations for locating these new facilities were based at least in part on their predictions concerning the geographical distribution of the city's population in 1980. As figure 2.2 shows, those predictions were not terribly accurate. (The figure uses the same geographical breakdown that was used in table 2.1 and in the map in figure 2.1.) The framers of the 1960 Plan made their most glaring errors in predicting substantial population increases for Center City, Southwest Philadelphia, and Germantown-Chestnut Hill, when in fact all of these sections actually lost population between 1950 and 1980. For the inner city ring surrounding the central business district, the planners correctly foresaw the direction of change (that is, downward), but they seriously underestimated the magnitude of the population losses. The two inner city sections where they predicted stability—West Philadelphia and Kensington—both lost about a third of their populations over the thirty-year period. Similarly, the losses in South Philadelphia, Lower and Upper North Philadelphia were far greater than the planners had foreseen. Even in the sections where the planners accurately projected increases—(Roxborough-Manayunk, Olney-Oak Lane, the Near and Far Northeast)—the actual gains fell far short of those anticipated. Errors of this magnitude in predicting the size and distribution of the city's population must surely call into question the plan's recommendations for building community facilities to serve that population.

## POSTREFORM POLITICS

One of the historic ironies in Philadelphia's postwar planning is that the long-awaited Comprehensive Plan was produced just as the decade of political reform was coming to a close. The plan is therefore more accurately described as the culmination of the reform period rather than the point of departure for a new era of planning. It expressed the vision of the like-minded coalition of politicians, professionals, businessmen and financiers who dominated Philadelphia politics in the 1950s. They constituted a classic example of the progrowth coalition that was common to many American cities in the postwar era. Yet their grip on municipal government was tenuous, and gave way in the early 1960s to a more traditional style of machine politics. Much of the literature on progrowth coalitions in American cities seems to assume that they maintained a constant presence on the development scene throughout the postwar period. In Philadelphia that is clearly not the case. In fact, organized business elites had a very uneven record of political activism during the postwar years. At no

**Figure 2.2**
**Predicted and Actual Population Change**
**1950-1980**

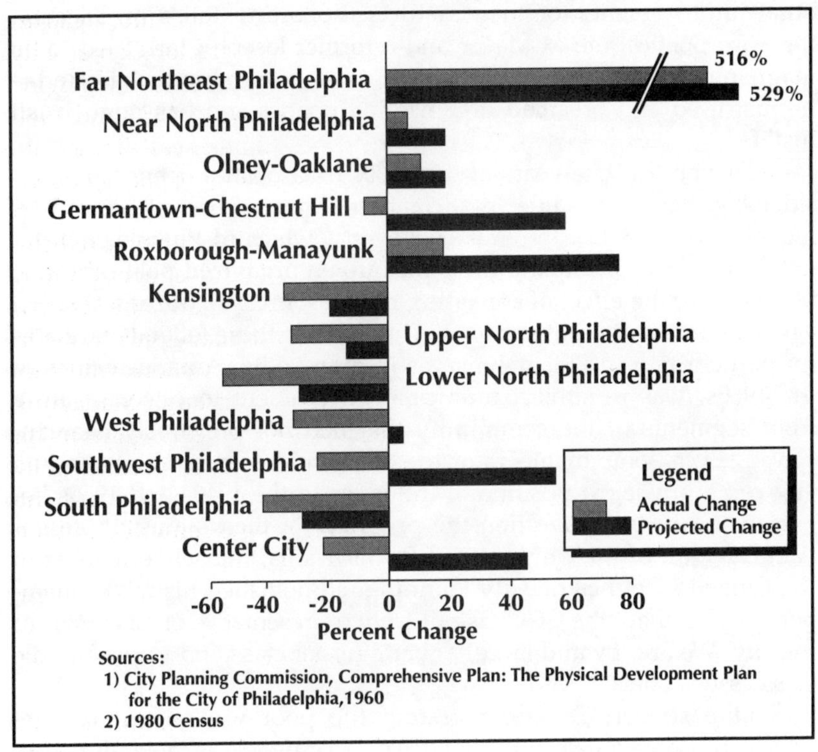


time after the 1950s did they play so central a role in development as they did during the reform years.

In February 1962, only six months after the city council had formally endorsed the plan as "a comprehensive and proper guide for the physical development of the city," reformer Richardson Dilworth resigned as mayor in order to campaign for governor. His successor was Philadelphia's first Irish-Catholic mayor, James Tate, a ward politician whose constituency was decidedly different from that of the reformers who preceded him. During Tate's ten years in office (1962 to 1971), his strongest allies were the city's white ethnic groups and labor unions, particularly the public employees. Mayor Tate practiced old-fashioned machine politics of the kind his predecessors deplored. Tate revived patronage at the municipal level, distributing jobs to reward the party's faithful. Nor was he averse to compensating his supporters in city council with public works: new swimming pools, street lighting, or other improvements for their districts. Reflecting Tate's predilection for ward politics, the ex-Mayor and reformer Joseph Clark tried to be magnanimous: "his problems are, to some extent, his background—he just lived and breathed organization politics and has done so all his life."[34]

During the Tate years of the 1960s local politics opened up considerably, due to the new participation requirements introduced by federal programs like the War on Poverty, which in Philadelphia did not succeed in galvanizing the poor into an organized political force, but did have the effect of spreading new resources to dozens of social agencies and community groups. The effect of these federal mandates for participation in Philadelphia, as in many other American cities in the 1960s, was to subject municipal government to closer scrutiny from segments of the community that had not previously been involved. Even some members of the civic and business elite who had enjoyed a privileged position of influence in the 1940s and 1950s began in the 1960s to question the propriety of their status. Professor Paul Davidoff of the University of Pennsylvania, himself a member of the Citizens' Council on City Planning, admonished his fellow members in 1965 that "the CCCP is not truly representative of all classes in the city. We are, by and large, a white upper class and upper middle class association."[35]

One strategy for incorporating the poor was to put college-educated professionals in the service of poor people as their advocates. Not only in the legal system, but in the realm of urban planning as well, the idea gained ground that in order to participate, the poor needed to be represented by the very same expertise that had traditionally served elite interests. The city planning commission, whose staff included former VISTA and Peace Corps volunteers, adopted a modified version of advocacy planning by creating in the late 1960s a new district planning structure, with each of the various sections of the city getting its own community planner. This new structure mirrored a more "distributed" approach to the city's redevelopment, downplaying large-scale urban renewal projects and stressing instead the conservation of large numbers of neighborhoods across the city.[36]

By and large, however, Philadelphia's civic elite in the 1960s was "more concerned with attacking the economic problems of the poor than in heightening their political participation."[37] Nowhere is this more evident than in the political fortunes of the city's blacks during that turbulent decade. As in other American cities, blacks in Philadelphia demonstrated, picketed, and organized boycotts. Each time the objective was tangible and immediate: the investigation of labor union hiring practices, stepped-up inspections of housing violations, bussing that threatened a black neighborhood. But these discrete acts of protest did not often produce lasting political gains.[38] The federally sponsored antipoverty program "never encouraged independent political activities that could significantly affect traditional power relationships in Philadelphia politics."[39] In fact, Mayor Tate used the program as an extension of the party organization, pressuring antipoverty workers to campaign for his reelection in 1967. Tate's representatives to the antipoverty board often made policy and communicated it directly to the executive director, bypassing the board's grassroots members.[40] Yet throughout the decade of the 1960s, black voters supported Tate's Democratic organization consistently and overwhelmingly.[41]

Unlike his two reform-minded predecessors, Tate found himself constantly embroiled in feuds with the city's business community. A 1970 study commissioned by the United States Department of Housing and Urban Development charged that an "unnecessary gulf" separated Mayor Tate's administration from the "business power structure," because neither side was willing to cooperate on common goals.[42] Moreover, Tate lost the support of white liberals and reformers early in his tenure, and by the time he ran for reelection in 1967 there was open feuding in the Democratic City Committee between those two wings of the party. Although the liberals managed to deny Tate the party's official endorsement in the primary, Tate won anyway, supported by labor unions, especially the municipal employees' unions. In the general election most of the city's business leaders, organized within the Greater Philadelphia Movement, supported Tate's Republican opponent. When he narrowly won reelection, Mayor Tate broke off relations with the business community.

During his second term Tate alienated yet another important Democratic constituency by sounding an increasingly strident theme of law and order. His appointment of Frank Rizzo as police commissioner, while it cemented the loyalty of working-class and middle-class white ethnics, repelled blacks. When Frank Rizzo himself campaigned to succeed Tate as mayor, he capitalized on his image as a tough cop to win the support of "rowhouse Philadelphia," while causing black voters virtually to abandon the Democratic ticket.

Philadelphia entered the 1970s with a majority party badly splintered, and Rizzo's two terms did little to put it back together. Relying almost exclusively on his support among white ethnics, Mayor Rizzo made no effort to woo disaffected white liberals or blacks back to the Democratic Party. Indeed, he seemed to have little regard for party alignments at all, endorsing the Republican Richard Nixon in the 1972 presidential election. An added burden for the party was the feud between Rizzo and state-level Democrats, which began when Democratic Governor Milton Shapp delivered a dramatic, last-minute endorsement to Rizzo's opponent in the primary race. The city party was in internal disarray, enjoying the cooperation of neither state-level nor national-level Democrats.

In this fragmented environment, neighborhood groups gathered strength and visibility in the 1970s as a citywide political force. Not that neighborhood organization was new to Philadelphia in the 1970s. Far from it. The city had a history of civic activism within communities. Table 2.2 shows the distribution throughout the city of neighborhood civic organizations established in the 1950s and 1960s. It shows that the level of community organizing, already high in the 1950s,

**Table 2.2**

Neighborhood Civic Organizations in Philadelphia, by Major Section of the City*, 1950s and 1960s

| | *Organizations Begun in 1950s* | *Organizations Begun in 1960s* |
|---|---|---|
| Center City | 4 | 4 |
| South Philadelphia | 15 | 22 |
| Southwest Philadelphia | 6 | 11 |
| West Philadelphia | 11 | 26 |
| Western North Philadelphia | 10 | 21 |
| Eastern North Philadelphia | 6 | 15 |
| Roxborough-Manayunk | 5 | 7 |
| Germantown-Chestnut Hill | 22 | 31 |
| Near Northeast Philadelphia | 26 | 23 |
| Far Northeast Philadelphia | 13 | 19 |

*Note that the sections of the city used in this table are somewhat different from those in table 2.1. North Philadelphia is divided into eastern and western sections, instead of upper and lower, and the neighborhoods of Kensington and Olney-Oaklane have been folded into other sections.

*Source:* William Cutler and Howard Gillette, eds., *The Divided Metropolis* (Westport, Conn.: Greenwood Press, 1980), p. 274.

accelerated in the 1960s. With few exceptions, however, these organizations addressed themselves only to local-level issues involving housing, zoning, recreation and schools. Rarely did they apply themselves to any wider political agenda.[43]

The important departure of the 1970s was the formation of a citywide coalition. In 1973 twelve neighborhood associations banded together to establish a citywide Council of Neighborhood Organizations whose membership and influence expanded each year. One of its major functions was to act as a watchdog over the city's budget and programs, to see that neighborhood services and public works received their fair share of municipal resources. Federal funding sources remained a strong influence on city policies in the 1970s, although the administration of Mayor Frank Rizzo was involved in constant skirmishes with federal officials over the use of federal funds. (The longest-running of these skirmishes was with the United States Department of Housing and Urban Development, which periodically accused the Rizzo administration in Philadelphia of discriminating against minority neighborhoods in its use of Community Development Funds, and on several occasions actually withheld grants from the city to try to force compliance.)

As for the downtown business community, its relationship to Frank Rizzo was at first mixed, but deteriorated dramatically in his second term. In his first mayoral campaign Rizzo got off to a bad start with the Greater Philadelphia Movement by refusing to respond to a questionnaire they distributed to all mayoral candidates. He asserted that he would not allow the city's business elite to interfere in the electoral process, but instead would go directly to the people. But once in office, Rizzo earned at least lukewarm support from many business people by holding the line on taxes throughout his first term (1971–1975).

Immediately after his reelection to a second term, however, Mayor Rizzo announced an $86 million deficit that forced him to ask for a thirty percent increase in both the personal property tax and the real estate tax. When the Chamber of Commerce accused him of deliberately concealing the deficit to get reelected, Mayor Rizzo responded by blaming the city's economic problems on the "ineffectuality" of the city's business executives—a reply that widened the gap between business and the mayor. The antipathy business leaders felt toward the mayor was demonstrated in their solid opposition to his bid in 1978 for a change in the city charter that would have allowed him to run for a third term. Funds supplied by the business community paid for a successful voter registration drive in the city's black neighborhoods and for radio advertisements. The charter change was soundly defeated.

Not all of the decline in business activism in the 1970s was due to the mayor's stance. The business community of the 1970s was itself more fragmented, less organized, and less committed to specific development initiatives than it had been in the 1950s. By the 1970s, Philadelphia had declined as a headquarters city, and many of the city's leading executives were the heads of branch offices whose primary loyalty was to their corporate headquarters in other cities rather than to Philadelphia. They were therefore less committed to specific projects and less inclined to offer their organized backing to the city's development efforts. To sum up, the political environment of the city became more and more fragmented during the 1960s and 1970s, as a once-unified civic and governmental elite gave way to a complicated mosaic of interest groups, among whom business people were less prominent than they had been in the 1950s.

## IMPLEMENTING CAPITAL PLANS

The splintering of the Democratic party was increasingly reflected in the absence of party discipline within the city council and the lack of coordination between the council and the city administration. Although they continued to wear the Democratic label, members of the council developed their own financial and electoral bases, independent of the party. Although mayors remained the titular head of their party, they exercised less and less leverage over other party politicians. One important consequence of this lapse in organizational discipline has been the widening gap between capital budgets passed by the council and the actual construction of capital projects. For evidence of that gap we need only compare the annual capital budgets of the 1970s with the building programs that followed from them. Here we are talking, not about how closely a twenty-year scheme corresponds to subsequent development, but rather how well the annual appropriation for capital projects conforms to the construction that is undertaken in the succeeding year. Figure 2.3 shows, for the decade of the 1970s, the vast difference between the money that was appropriated in the annual capital budget for projects to be undertaken during the year ("appropriations") and the money that was actually spent in that same year

### Figure 2.3
### Capital Funding and Expenditures, by Budget Year
### (in millions of dollars)

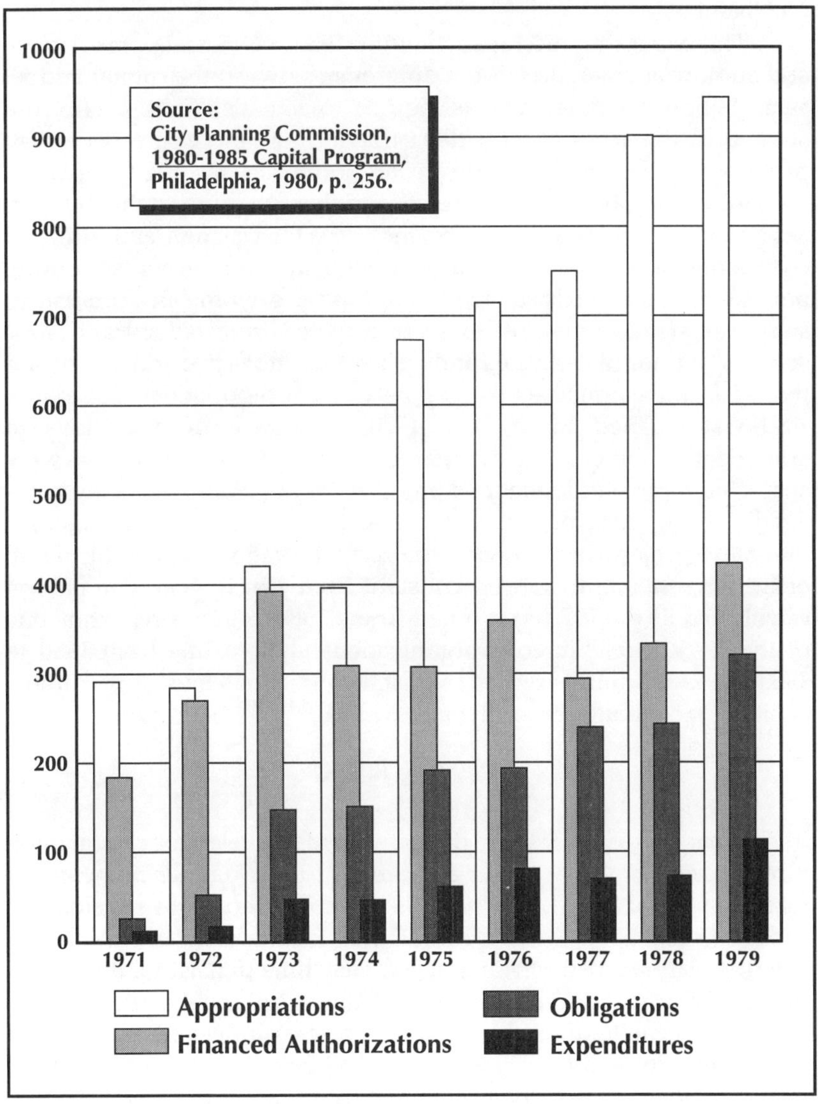

("expenditures"). The figure also portrays the two steps that intervene between the initial appropriation and the ultimate expenditure, the first being the money that was actually made available during the year by the city for spending ("authorizations"), and the second being the money that was formally committed by contract for specific projects ("obligations").

The increasing discrepancy in the 1970s between appropriations and authorizations reflected the difference between the capital budget as a political document and as a guide to actual spending. The constant pressure from all city departments for new and replacement projects, coupled with the desire for more facilities on the part of neighborhood lobbies, dictated a constantly expanding capital budget. Yet by the late 1970s the city's finance director was tightening control over actual spending by city departments and was, in effect, opting not to spend some of the money appropriated by the city council. In some cases funds that had been anticipated from federal and state sources did not materialize, and hence, the projects could not be authorized. Interestingly, as the gap between appropriations and authorizations widened in the late 1970s, the ratio of obligations to authorizations increased. Apparently, as city departments were subjected to greater limitations on what they could spend, they managed to bring more of their authorized projects to the contract stage. Once the projects were under contract, the ratio of expenditures to obligations was comparatively constant from year to year. The pattern established in the 1970s continued in the 1980s. A 1984 report by one of the city's public interest organizations showed that from 1980 to 1983 the city administration obligated only about half of its annual capital appropriation from the city council.[44]

## CONCLUSION

In the years since 1945, then, the nature of Philadelphia's capital planning process has changed significantly. In the decade immediately following World War II, that process was characterized by consultation within a very narrow circle of influential Philadelphians, with the result that planners had a comparatively easy time translating their ideas into physical reality. The simple and direct link between plans and outcomes began to unravel in the 1960s, as new influences from within the community and from the federal level entered the scene. The annual capital budget gradually changed in character, from an appropriation bill to fund those projects on which there was agreement to proceed, to a symbolic reassurance to all of the various municipal departments and competing community interests that their voices were being heard by the mayor and council. Council members from every district in the city pressed to have their constituents' projects included in the annual budget, and there existed no central party leadership strong enough to make and enforce choices about which projects would be included and which ones excluded. As a result, an increasing number of projects each year were incorporated, but not constructed. The obvious conclusion to be drawn is that the locus of decision about which projects actually get built has shifted to a later point in the process. Rather then being thrashed out before the mayor's submission of the capital budget to the city council, or even during the council's deliberations, many of the choices among competing alternatives are now being made after the budget is adopted, when the city administration decides how much of the appropriated funds it really intends to spend.

Given the obvious gap between plans and real outcomes, it seems desirable that we refrain from trying to evaluate the city's priorities by examining its formal capital plans, and try instead to discover what the pattern of actual spending has been in Philadelphia in the postwar period. Hence, I shall move in the next chapter to a review of the distribution of capital expenditures on certain types of community facilities during the thirty-year period from 1950 to 1979.

# The Distribution of Community Improvements

IN the first chapter of this volume, we examined several different theories that have been used to explain the distribution of public improvements in American cities. Pluralist theory stresses the role that politics plays in determining where new facilities will be built and old ones expanded, concluding that because poor and minority neighborhoods are less organized and less influential in local politics, they are likely to be at a disadvantage in getting their share of public works. Neo- Marxists have argued that the lack of investment in the declining parts of inner cities is due to the perception on the part of capitalist elites (and the public authorities who do the elites' bidding) that those neighborhoods are increasingly marginal to the production of wealth and that the residents are therefore less entitled to "social wages" in the form of the public facilities. Still a third model emphasizes economic rationality as the explanation for municipal decisions to allocate public investments; the best example is the triage model, according to which policy makers select areas for investment by estimating where those investments are likely to yield the greatest payoffs. Poor and minority neighborhoods lose out in this model as well, because they are so often regarded as poor investment risks. Although they offer quite different explanations for the low levels of public investment in the inner city, the proponents of all of these theories start from the assumption that such public disinvestment has in fact occurred, and that local governments have systematically shortchanged the areas inhabited by poor and minority residents.

Yet the brief historical overview of Philadelphia's reform tradition in the last chapter raises questions about this assumption regarding public disinvestment. Some of the business and civic leaders who guided Philadelphia's postwar redevelopment in the 1950s shared the long-standing (and perhaps paternalistic) belief of earlier reformers, that public works offered one path to the social reconstruction of the poor. Their plans for the redevelopment of the city therefore included significant investments in some of the poorest parts of Philadelphia. To the extent that such plans were carried out, they should have produced an investment pattern that is different from the one predicted by the various disinvestment theories outlined in chapter 1.

How well does disinvestment theory fit the actual pattern of public investment in Philadelphia in the postwar period? To explore that question, I have used data on capital spending from 1950 to 1979 for five different types of community facilities throughout Philadelphia neighborhoods: (1) recreation projects, including playgrounds, parks, and pools, (2) police stations, (3) fire stations, (4) branch libraries, and (5) public schools. These particular types of spending were chosen because their results are highly visible in the neighborhoods, unlike some other forms of capital spending (for example, money spent on street paving or utility lines). Furthermore, all five indisputably represent assets to the communities in which they are located; the same cannot be said for some other types of capital spending (for example, on public housing). Finally, the most important criterion for choosing these particular services was that they are services commonly used by all income groups and all races. Thus, we might reasonably expect them to be widely distributed throughout neighborhoods of various income levels and races. This is an important assumption, because it distinguishes my study from a number of others that have investigated the location of social service facilities that are specifically intended to assist disadvantaged clients. Such studies have found (not surprisingly) that those facilities are heavily concentrated in poor, minority areas.[1]

The first step in discovering how the city had distributed its investments in community improvements was to group census tracts in the city of Philadelphia into 104 "neighborhoods." My major criteria in designing these groupings were three. First, each group of tracts had to constitute an identifiable neighborhood with a name that is a meaningful designation, not just to its own residents, but to other Philadelphians as well. While it might be difficult to subdivide some American cities on this basis, Philadelphia is self-consciously a "city of neighborhoods" in which commonly accepted boundaries and labels for neighborhoods are used constantly by real estate agents, politicians, journalists, and Philadelphians in general, to organize the sociopolitical space within the city limits.[2] Second, each tract grouping had to have its land occupied primarily by residential development rather than industrial, commercial, warehouse, and port facilities, major city parks, or other nonresidential uses. Third, my tract groupings had to have consistent boundaries across the 1950, 1960, 1970, and 1980 censuses, so that trends could be charted.[3]

Neighborhoods differ quite markedly in size, because of the physical boundaries and social attributes which define them. Thus, although the average neighborhood in my sample had fifteen thousand residents in 1980, the populations ranged from only a few thousand to as many as thirty-five thousand. Size, however, is not the only dimension on which they differ. The tremendous variation among the city's neighborhoods on almost all socioeconomic indicators is one of the most striking and oft-observed characteristics of Philadelphia. In fact, one study of the mid-1970s asserted that "with the exception of New York City, Philadelphia is probably the most socially-heterogeneous city in the United States," and went on to argue that the tendency of Philadelphians to translate social differences into spatial segregation is a major cause of conflict in the city.[4] America's big cities have always displayed significant differences in wealth from neighborhood to neighborhood. In Philadelphia since World War II, discrepancies between rich and poor neighborhoods have persisted, judging by the figures in table 3.1.

Two concurrent movements taking place during this same period have made the contrasts between wealthy and poor neighborhoods all the more striking. I refer to the continuing deterioration of some poor and working-class areas near the center of the city, while at the same time a process of gentrification has transformed neighboring areas into high-rent districts. An example of this situation is depicted in figure 3.1, showing four neighborhoods near the center of the city

**Table 3.1**

Maximum and Minimum Values of Median Household Income, for 104
Philadelphia Neighborhoods

| | | | | Dollar Difference between Highest and Lowest | |
| | | | | --- | --- |
| Year | Highest Household Income | Lowest Household Income | Ratio of Highest to Lowest | In Unadjusted Dollars | In Constant Dollars |
| --- | --- | --- | --- | --- | --- |
| 1950 | $ 5,678 | $ 890 | 6.4 | $ 4,788 | $6,641 |
| 1960 | 7,813 | 1,492 | 5.2 | 6,321 | 7,126 |
| 1970 | 13,929 | 3,185 | 4.4 | 10,744 | 9,238 |
| 1980 | 23,317 | 5,164 | 4.5 | 18,153 | 7,355 |

whose fortunes have diverged dramatically. All four were at the low
end of the income scale in 1950. But two of them, Fairmount and
Spring Garden, have undergone considerable gentrification, especially
in the 1970s. By 1980 both of these "renaissance" neighborhoods had
become middle-class enclaves. At the same time, the areas immediately north and east were declining even further, so that by 1980 their
populations had the lowest incomes of any neighborhoods in the entire city.

In addition to variations in income, Philadelphia's neighborhoods differ dramatically along racial and ethnic lines, the most important cleavage being, of course, between black and white
neighborhoods. During the postwar period, the proportion of the
city's population that was black doubled, from under twenty percent
in 1950 to almost forty percent in 1980. The increase in the size of the
black population was accompanied by an increase in residential segregation, measured by Taeuber's index of dissimilarity.[5] Interestingly,
neighborhoods dominated by whites and blacks sometimes exist side
by side, with impenetrable racial boundaries separating them. This
situation exists, for example, in South Philadelphia, where working-
class Italian enclaves persist in an otherwise black section of the city.
Farther north, the Polish and Irish neighborhoods of Kensington and
Fishtown directly adjoin, but do not interact with, several black communities of North Philadelphia. In short, the growth of the city's black
population since 1950 has not led to a homogenization of Philadelphia's neighborhoods; on the contrary, it has been accompanied by
increased separation of the races.

For information on capital expenditures, my primary data
sources were the Philadelphia City Planning Commission and the

**Figure 3.1**
**Four Contiguous Neighborhoods in Center City**

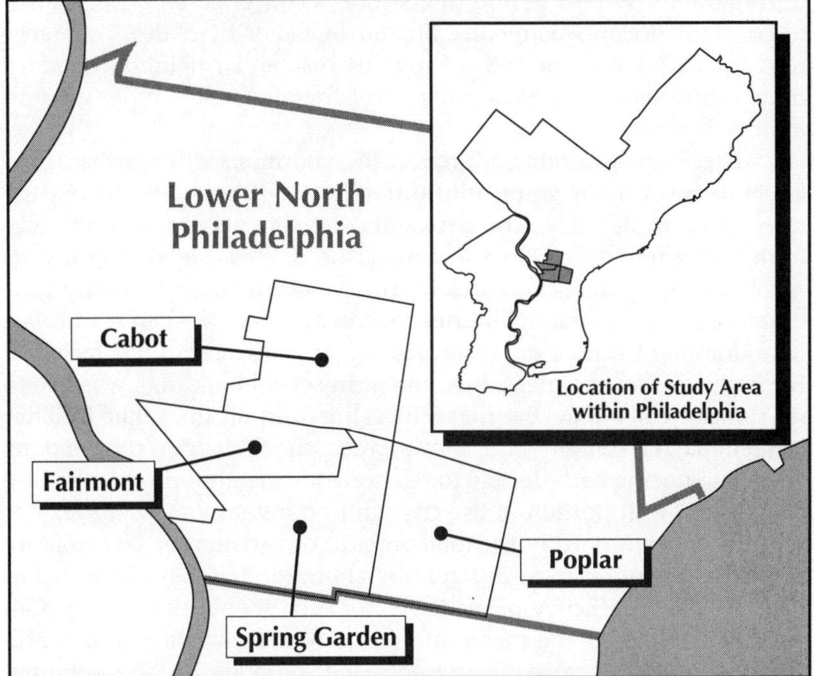


Philadelphia School District (the latter maintains a bureaucracy and a budget that are separate from city government in Philadelphia). Because public expenditures on capital facilities occur in large "lumps," it is possible to detect patterns only in the distribution of such expenditures over extended time periods. Looking at the share of funds going to a particular neighborhood in a particular year, or even over five years, cannot give a meaningful indication of the city's longer-term spending practices, since even the most favored neighborhoods are bound to experience years of little or no investment. Hence, I decided to track investments over three decades. The Planning Commission supplied data on the cost of every police and fire station, library, and recreation facility that was built or substantially rehabilitated between 1950 and 1979, while the school district provided expenditure figures for all schools that were either constructed or expanded during the same period. Having mapped the locations of all of these projects,

I assigned the expenditures for each one to the neighborhood in which it was located. Because inflation was so pronounced at certain times during the thirty-year period in question, I converted all expenditures to constant dollars, using the Bureau of Labor Statistics' consumer price index.[6] Thus, for each of my 104 residential neighborhoods, I have a thirty-year record of public investments for five types of community facilities.

The figures in table 3.2 reflect the enormous differences in the levels of investment going into different neighborhoods during the three postwar decades. The per capita investments range all the way from only a few dollars to a few thousand dollars. Separating investments made by the school district from those made by the city government (i.e., recreation, libraries, police, and fire), we can readily see how dominant school expenditures are among community facilities. For each decade, the mean investment in school buildings was five to six times greater than the mean investment in all the other facilities combined. As column one shows, the school district confined its spending during each decade to relatively few neighborhoods, leaving a substantial proportion of the city with no investment whatever.

In order to portray the total amount of variation or dissimilarity in the treatment given to different neighborhoods, I have included in table 3.2 the "coefficient of variation" for each spending category. Calculated by dividing the mean into the standard deviation, this coefficient is useful because it presents the variation in the different categories in a standardized form. It thus gives us a way to compare the different categories to one another. The smaller the coefficient, the less variation exists in per capita spending.[7] The table reveals an interesting fact about spending patterns in the 1960s; there was apparently a move in that decade toward a more even distribution of investments across the city. The data for city spending during the decade of the 1960s show the smallest coefficient of variation on the table, along with a slight increase in the percentage of neighborhoods receiving investments, and the smallest range of difference between lowest and highest investments. Evidently, the city administration in the 1960s spread its investments more widely and evenly than they have been distributed either before or since then, confirming the characterization of Mayor Tate's administration as one practicing traditional pork barrel politics. Even the school district, while it showed substantial variation in the dollars invested in different neighborhoods during the 1960s, nevertheless spread its investments to a dramatically

**Table 3.2**

The Distribution of Per Capita Investments in Community Facilities in 104 Philadelphia Neighborhoods*

| | *Percentage of Neighborhoods Receiving Funds* | *Lowest Amount ($/cap.)* | *Highest Amount ($/cap.)* | *Mean Amount ($/cap.)* | *Standard Deviation* | *Coefficient of Variation (Standard Deviation/ Mean)* |
|---|---|---|---|---|---|---|
| Schools | | | | | | |
| 1950s | 36% | $1.65 | $2,229.09 | $282.99 | $472.83 | 1.67 |
| 1960s | 63% | 2.13 | 2,240.63 | 189.00 | 351.97 | 1.86 |
| 1970s | 39% | 4.86 | 1,671.26 | 217.75 | 313.23 | 1.44 |
| City Facilities | | | | | | |
| 1950s | 76% | 1.67 | 1,939.74 | 47.18 | 217.65 | 4.61 |
| 1960s | 78% | 1.02 | 214.50 | 34.34 | 41.76 | 1.22 |
| 1970s | 68% | .76 | 937.00 | 43.77 | 118.55 | 2.71 |

**Note:* Dollar values converted to their 1967 level using the Bureau of Labor Statistics' consumer price index.

larger proportion of all neighborhoods than it has ever done, before or since (see column 1 of table 3.2).

## NEIGHBORHOOD INCOME AND COMMUNITY IMPROVEMENTS

One way to test the validity of disinvestment theories is to compare the treatment received by poor and minority neighborhoods with that received by better-off neighborhoods during the postwar years. We begin with some crosstabulations of median income with capital investments in community facilities. For each of the three postwar decades, our 104 neighborhoods are divided approximately into thirds, according to the neighborhood's median household income—lowest-income, middle-income, and highest- income.[8]

Table 3.3 shows how neighborhoods at the various income levels fared in each of the three decades with respect to the total investments made by the city and school district in the five types of facilities in question. In the 1950s more than half of the lowest-income neighborhoods got only low investments or none at all, and only two of the poor neighborhoods received the highest level of investment. That pattern

**Table 3.4**

Neighborhoods of Philadelphia, Classified by Racial Composition and by Level of Investment in Community Facilities

| Level of Investment Going into Neighborhood | Racial Composition of Neighborhood | | | | | | | | |
| --- | --- | --- | --- | --- | --- | --- | --- | --- | --- |
| | 1950–1959 | | | 1960–1969 | | | 1970–1979 | | |
| | *Nonwhite* | *Mixed* | *White* | *Nonwhite* | *Mixed* | *White* | *Nonwhite* | *Mixed* | *White* |
| High investment | 0 | 2 | 15 | 6 | 2 | 13 | 8 | 6 | 3 |
| Medium investment | 4 | 6 | 25 | 6 | 15 | 26 | 12 | 4 | 13 |
| Low investment | 6 | 6 | 40 | 3 | 5 | 28 | 7 | 12 | 39 |
| | 10 | 14 | 80 | 15 | 22 | 67 | 27 | 22 | 55 |

neighborhoods falling into those three categories changed significantly over the course of 30 years, with the number of predominantly white areas declining as the number of predominantly minority areas increased—from only 10 in 1950, to 15 in 1960, and 27 in 1970. (Interestingly, however, the same number of neighborhoods fell into the "mixed" category in the 1960s and the 1970s.)

The figures show that in the 1950s over half of the minority enclaves got little or no investment, while none received a high level of investment. The treatment of minority neighborhoods improved considerably in the 1960s, when most of them received either moderate or high levels of investment. We notice some improvement as well in the treatment of the mixed areas in the 1960s; while only two of them received a high rate of investment, many more neighborhoods found themselves in the moderate investment category than had been the case in the 1950s. Nor do the gains made by the minority areas appear to have come at the expense of white areas, which did about as well as they had in the earlier decade. Yet again, the data portray the 1960s as a period of widespread investment in community facilities across all types of neighborhoods.

Predominantly white areas and mixed neighborhoods received far less favorable treatment in the 1970s, suggesting that an important shift of resources took place in the 1970s, withdrawing investments from the white and mixed communities while maintaining, or even improving, the treatment extended to the minority sections of the city.

An analysis of the city's spending on recreation facilities in the 1970s suggests that the favoritism extended to minority communities came, not so much in the formulation of the capital budget as in its implementation. That is, minority neighborhoods in the 1970s were more likely to see proposed projects implemented than were other neighborhoods. Table 3.5 shows the completion rates for projects in nonwhite neighborhoods to have been higher than completion rates in either mixed or white neighborhoods. When it came down to matching dollars with projects, the city administration showed a stronger commitment to inner city projects than to others.

The picture that emerges from the expenditure data is decidedly *not* that of public investments being gradually siphoned away from the low-income and minority sections of the city. Granted, the allocation of investments from 1950 to 1959 appears to have favored the highest-income areas and those that were predominantly white. But the figures for the more recent decades portray an investment pattern that became increasingly favorable to low-income and minority neighborhoods.

Perhaps the best example of this distributive pattern is the city's record of investment in Lower North Philadelphia, consistently the poorest part of the city since World War II (see figure 3.2). Stretching two a half miles north from the edge of downtown, and three miles across from the Delaware to the Schuylkill River, Lower North Philadelphia presents the classic case of a once-vital industrial district of factories and homes from which businesses and families have fled, leaving behind abandoned plants, warehouses and homes, and overgrown lots piled high with trash. Table 3.6 shows the loss of almost 200,000 people since 1950, along with the change in the composition from predominantly white to nonwhite.

Throughout the postwar period city planners and redevelopment officials have fought an almost-constant battle against the forces of decay in this enclave of poverty. The very first slum area selected by Philadelphia officials for redevelopment under the federal Urban Renewal Program of 1949 was a section of Lower North Philadelphia known as East Poplar, where the city had the distinction in 1952 of completing the first Title I project in the nation. Two Quaker organizations, with the help of the city redevelopment authority, transformed a series of dilapidated old buildings into 174 cooperative garden apartments. That same year the city acquired a nearby tract and again made history by being the first authority to use Title I funds for public housing. In rapid succession the city acquired dozens of parcels in North Philadelphia, turning them over to developers for the construction of public and private housing, and to Temple University for its expansion.

**Table 3.5**

Completion Rates on Recreation Projects Proposed in Mayor Rizzo's First Three Capital Budgets (1972, 1973, 1974)

|  | *Nonwhite Areas* | *Mixed Areas* | *White Areas* |
|---|---|---|---|
| Number of neighborhoods in the city | 31 | 24 | 49 |
| Number of projects proposed | 31 | 29 | 41 |
| Number of projects completed* | 15 | 9 | 17 |
| Percentage completed | 48% | 31% | 40% |

*Note:* A project was defined as "completed" if it had been built by 1979, the end of Mayor Rizzo's term in office. Recognizing the time lags involved in building capital projects, I chose to track only Mayor Rizzo's early capital budgets because they had the highest probability of being completed by the end of his term.

**Figure 3.2**
**Lower North Philadelphia**

In 1966, when Congress established the ill-fated Model Cities Program to promote greater coordination between cities' physical rebuilding efforts and their social services, Philadelphia responded by designating Lower North Philadelphia as its one and only Model Cities target area. The program ran into serious problems involving political conflict between the staff and community groups, as well as charges of mismanagement. It dissolved within only a few years, leaving behind only murky records of its efforts and accomplishments. Yet it undoubtedly made an important contribution to Lower North Philadelphia by establishing a set of expectations and commitments that extended well beyond its own lifetime. The city's commitment to use subsequent federal moneys to complete projects started under Model Cities meant that Lower North Philadelphia retained its priority position on the city's redevelopment agenda even after the Model Cities program faded.

With the advent of the Community Development Block Grant (CDBG) program of 1974 as a replacement for urban renewal, Model Cities, and several other federal subsidy programs, Philadelphia again opted for continuity. Within the first several years of the CDBG program, the city had designated a total of 44 "neighborhood strategy areas," a third of them within the boundaries of Lower North Philadelphia (which contained only 6% of the city's total land area).

To complement the variety of federal redevelopment programs targeted to Lower North Philadelphia, the city spent substantial amounts of money on modern community facilities, which they saw not only as responses to demand for services but also as contributors to neighborhood renewal. Table 3.7 shows the proportion of the city's investments going into Lower North Philadelphia during the three postwar decades, separating out the expenditures for recreation and schools as the two most important components of the total. During the 1950s and 1960s the school district was more generous to this area than were recreation planners, a situation that was reversed during the 1970s. Yet overall expenditures climbed steadily upward, a trend that is particularly striking because of the population losses suffered by this area during the decades in question. In 1950 Lower North Philadelphia contained 18% of the city's population and got 20% of its investments during the 1950s; by 1970 it housed only 12% of the population yet captured 27% of the investments made during the 1970s. Once again, we have a finding that does not easily square with the disinvestment theories outlined in chapter 1.

Nor does it square with some expenditure models that portray

**Table 3.7**
Share of Investments in Community Facilities Going to Lower North Philadelphia

|  | *1950–1959* | *1960–1969* | *1970–1979* |
|---|---|---|---|
| Investments in recreation | 14% | 9% | 31% |
| Investments in schools | 21% | 24% | 26% |
| All facilities combined | 20% | 22% | 27% |

municipal facilities planners as operating chiefly on the basis of demand for services. This is the portrait painted in a study of Philadelphia's capital spending in the 1950s and 1960s, whose author emphasized population growth, population density, and inadequate capacity as the main factors driving capital spending. In effect, he argued that public planners tend to respond to demand, generated either by increasing concentrations of population in older neighborhoods whose facilities have become overcrowded, or by new development in outlying areas:

> Facility planners take the place of the private market when they decide how to distribute tax dollars among neighborhoods. Their job is to estimate demand for new facilities and to allocate available revenues among competing demands.[9]

But this explanation of facilities location cannot possibly account for the rising proportion of total investment that was captured by the inner city neighborhoods represented in table 3.6. The population decline suffered by those same areas would have reduced demand, rather than increasing it.

Furthermore, the data on capital expenditures are not easily reconciled with the pluralist model of politics, which assumes that poorer neighborhoods receive low levels of public investment because they lack political organization. According to pluralist theories, city politicians tend to channel investments into neighborhoods that contain their political supporters and hence, low-income neighborhoods can expect to be treated unfavorably until they organize to support and elect officeholders, who will then exchange benefits for their continued support.

It might be plausible to explain the treatment given to the low-income neighborhoods in the early 1950s and early 1960s on the basis of political considerations. After all, Mayor Joseph Clark, the first of the reform mayors of the 1950s, received only lukewarm electoral support from the low-income sections of the city. Although Clark won most of the West Philadelphia wards, he lost sixteen wards in North and South Central Philadelphia. Their lack of support might be seen as one explanation of why Mayor Clark spent less than the city average in these areas.

Following this line of reasoning, should we conclude that the electoral support given by these same areas to Mayor Tate's administration of the 1960s accounts for their somewhat better treatment during that decade? That is a debatable interpretation. Many observers of the Tate administration have concluded that Mayor Tate did little to curry favor within Philadelphia's black community, concentrating instead on white ethnic neighborhoods and labor unions as the heart of his constituency. One study of the city's experience with the War on Poverty found that "Tate and the civic elite implicitly relied on the political quiescence of Philadelphia's black community."[10] He took their votes for granted, and his confidence was justified. Even though his 1967 campaign for a second term focused on law and order, a theme that has traditionally offended black communities, he won heavily in the black wards. It seems doubtful, therefore, that the increases in capital spending in the poor black neighborhoods of the city should be seen as a deliberate part of Tate's electoral strategy.

If the pluralist model is questionable when applied to the 1960s, it is altogether untenable when applied to the 1970s. Our figures show that the low-income areas got relatively better treatment during Mayor Rizzo's administration than they had received during either of the previous decades. Yet these sections of the city voted heavily against Rizzo in 1971. Indeed, when we look at the wards won by Rizzo in 1971 (figure 3.3), we see that they do *not* include the low-income, minority communities of North Philadelphia, West Philadelphia and South Central Philadelphia. With only a few exceptions, these wards voted for Rizzo's Republican opponent. Their absence from the Rizzo camp was made all the more conspicuous by the fact that most of these same wards had heavily supported Mayor Tate in the 1967 election. Their switch to the Republican candidate in 1971 represented an anti-Rizzo vote.

If capital expenditures had been allocated according to the pluralist model, we would expect such a voting pattern to have produced a virtual withdrawal of funds by the Rizzo administration from the neighborhoods of West, North, and South Central Philadelphia. Instead, an important share of investments in community facilities went to those sections of the city that opposed Rizzo most strongly.


## EXPLAINING THE PATTERN OF INVESTMENTS


How can we account for this finding, which is altogether contrary to our expectations? Is it presaged by Lineberry's earlier study of location of public services in San Antonio? He, too, found that "it is the older,

**Figure 3.3**
**Wards Giving Majority to Frank Rizzo in 1971 Mayoral Election**

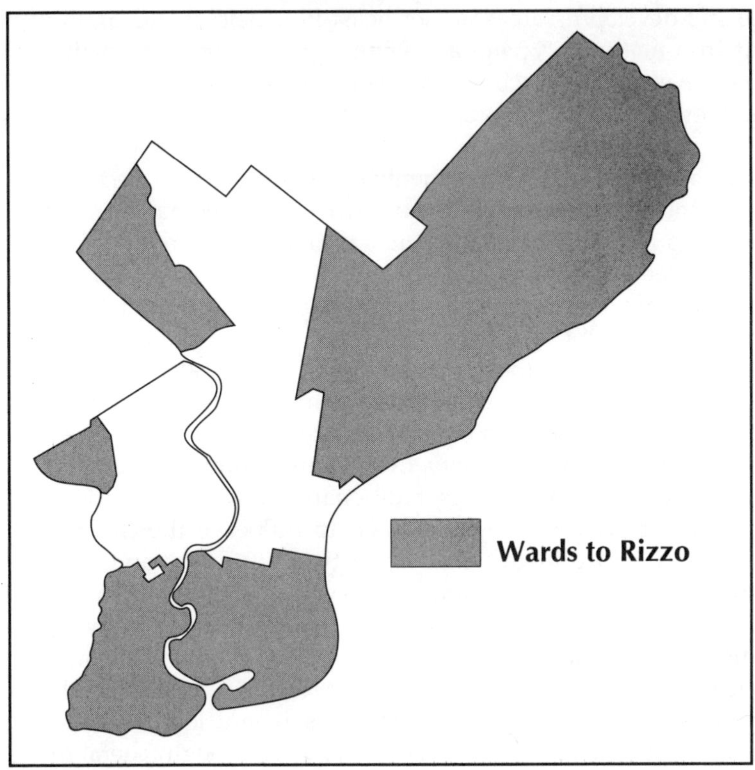


near-to-core areas which are consistently most proximate to public facilities."[11] The population of San Antonio was still growing in the 1960s, and Lineberry concluded that public works programs followed a concentric zone model of growth, with the construction of facilities lagging behind the population growth in newer, outlying areas. Hence, the older parts of town were better served, simply by virtue of their accumulated stock of community facilities. Yet Lineberry's interpretation of his findings, which rests on the historical advantage enjoyed by older neighborhoods, cannot adequately explain the Philadelphia data showing that poor neighborhoods have continued to receive more favorable treatment than more affluent areas of the city, right up to the most recent decade. The problem with applying Lineberry's hypothesis to Philadelphia is that he derived his interpretation from a city that was still in the process of developing. His theory that capital investments follow population growth is useful in explaining the massive investments that Philadelphia planners directed into the still-developing areas of Northeast Philadelphia during the 1950s. But in a mature city with a declining population and relatively little new development, such as Philadelphia was in the 1960s and 1970s, the view of capital investment as a response to new growth and demand is no longer applicable. We must search for some other way to explain the pattern of investments in the most recent decade.

One critical factor was the influence of the federal government on the city's redevelopment priorities. Federal urban renewal legislation encouraged local officials to combine housing programs with the construction of community facilities, giving cities the right to pay their one-third share of total project cost, not in cash, but by counting the community facilities they were building in renewal areas. Congress's Model Cities initiative of 1966 was another federal program that pressed cities to coordinate their housing efforts with the provision of social services in the inner city. Even though both Model Cities and the urban renewal program in its traditional form were suspended in 1973 by President Nixon, they continued to influence the city's building program because of the time lag between funding and completing various projects. The Community Development Block Grant (CDBG) program, created by Congress in 1974 to replace urban renewal, Model Cities and a number of other redevelopment programs, allowed cities to use federal funds for construction or rehabilitation of neighborhood facilities, so long as they served areas where low- and moderate-income households predominate. Thus, even though federal funds do not directly pay for the types of facilities we are considering, nevertheless the availability of federal funds for urban renewal and community development has encouraged cities to invest their own tax dollars in areas eligible for federal redevelopment funds—usually areas of poverty and minority concentrations.

Another factor contributing to the pattern of investments in the 1970 was the belt-tightening that occurred in the 1970s. Faced with shrinking city budgets, department heads appear to have reverted to a "worst-first" strategy, giving priority to the most urgent needs and all but withdrawing resources from the high-income areas of the city.[12] (Recall that table 3.3 shows very few high-income neighborhoods in the 1970s getting investments at either moderate or high levels.)

The most obvious reflection of this worst-first strategy was the shifting balance between building new projects and upgrading existing facilities. Philadelphia's capital budgets have always included both types of investment. In order to get continued payoffs from previous investments, additional funds must be periodically invested. Often, this happens when a facility has aged and needs to be readapted to fit contemporary requirements. For example, an older park or recreation center may need to be refurbished for new activities, particularly when the demographic structure of the neighborhood shifts significantly. Older facilities (e.g., police or fire stations) may need to be expanded to house larger staffs or new technology. Or older facilities may simply have deteriorated and need rehabilitation. In cases like these, capital planners face a choice between "writing off" the previous investment, or spending additional money, in order to get continued use from the facility. This kind of choice arises frequently in the older, inner-city neighborhoods where low-income residents are concentrated, and accounts for a portion of the capital invested there.

Additional constraints on the building of new facilities came in the decade of the 1970s in the form of tighter operating budgets. The construction of each new facility calls upon the operating budget to supply additional money for staff, supplies and equipment, heating and other utilities, and all of the other expenses connected with its operation. Improvements made to existing facilities, on the other hand, have a much smaller impact on operating budgets. As budget pressures mounted in the early 1970s, planners focused more attention on the increases in operating expenditures that would be generated by new buildings, a focus that led inevitably to the conclusion that a greater share of capital funds should be used to improve existing facilities.[13] Many older facilities in older parts of the city naturally benefited from such a shift in emphasis.

By comparing the spending records of Mayors Tate and Rizzo for recreation projects, we can easily detect the shift that occurred in the 1970s, from new construction to rehabilitation of existing sites. Mayor Tate's first three capital programs (1964, 1965, 1966) included a total of 92 recreation proposals, of which 65% represented new construction and only 35% were rehabilitations. By comparison, the recreation projects proposed in Mayor Rizzo's first three capital programs (1972, 1973, 1974) totaled 101, of which 48% were new construction and 53% involved rehabilitation. More important, when we consider how many of Rizzo's *proposed* projects were *actually constructed*, we find an even more pronounced emphasis on existing facilities: only 27% of the completed projects were new buildings, while fully 73% of completed projects involved rehabilitation.

In broad terms, the pattern of investments portrayed by my data conform to the three-part typology suggested by Norman and Susan Fainstein, a scheme that is reflected in the case studies presented in their collection, *Restructuring the City*.[14] The Fainsteins divide America's urban history since World War II into three different eras, each characterized by a particular type of local regime. Immediately following the war city governments emphasized large-scale public redevelopment that required clearance of slum neighborhoods and gave a strong guiding role to governmental planners. The governments of the period they label *directive* regimes. They were succeeded in the 1960s by *concessionary* regimes, whose allocation decisions were more favorable to minority-group and community interests. Starting in the 1970s they see a shift toward *conserving* regimes, whose policies reflect a priority on fiscal stability of local governments in the face of unfavorable economic trends.

The policy shifts the Fainsteins describe fit the Philadelphia situation reasonably well. During the 1950s a reform government closely aligned with civic and business leaders directed the renewal program and the drafting of the 1960 Comprehensive Plan with little popular opposition. While some civic groups were incorporated directly into the planning process, those groups were invariably elite organizations rather than representatives of lower-class communities. The mayor and planning commission deftly orchestrated the renewal effort from their center city offices. I have described the 1960s as a decade in which facilities were distributed more widely, giving more advantage to the poor and minority neighborhoods than they had enjoyed in the 1950s. And the Fainstein's label *conserving* might well be applied to the 1970s, when reductions in expenditures for community facilities became part of the city's response to increasing fiscal strains. The smaller number of dollars invested in such improvements was used to meet the worst emergencies, the majority of which involved patching up or expanding sites instead of building new ones.

It would be tempting to attribute these shifts in distributional patterns to increased political activism in the poor and minority neighborhoods, as the Fainsteins do. The *concessionary* regimes of the 1960s, they say, "were forced by the uprisings of the 1960s to be more responsive to lower-class interests than before or afterwards."[15] But the relationships between political support and public investment are not that direct. Philadelphia's poor black communities were politically supportive of the regime during the 1960s, mustering short-term resistance against specific construction projects or hiring practices, but consistently voting for Mayor Tate and his Democratic party regulars.

Rather than being a response to community activism, the shift toward a more distributive approach to community improvements was mainly a function of the overall shift in Philadelphia's redevelopment policy in the 1960s, away from large-scale clearance and toward preserving existing neighborhoods. Having started out with a policy of large-scale slum clearance of the most devastated areas, the city had by the late 1950s abandoned this strategy. A major study of the urban renewal program had recommended shifting away from this expensive clearance strategy, toward housing conservation in a much large number of neighborhoods. Public money needed to be spent to stem the spread of blight into vulnerable, though still-salvageable communities rather than to reclaim blocks that had already succumbed. As one account of the period reports, "Philadelphia early shied away from the bulldozer approach" and moved to "clearing only isolated blight and increasing public facilities such as parks and playgrounds, thus preserving areas that were salvageable."[16] This new emphasis on preserving neighborhoods led government to distribute resources more widely as opposed to concentrating them in a few very costly redevelopment sites. This was an approach that meshed well with the style of Mayor Tate and the Democratic party, in which pork- barrel politics had supplanted the reformist concerns of the 1950s. In short, the distributive approach of the 1960s was more a function of shifting planning approaches and machine politics than of urban unrest.

Nor does Philadelphia's experience in the 1970s fit altogether neatly into the Fainsteins' category of a *conserving* regime, one feature of which is its conservative political stance. Admittedly, Mayor Rizzo's appeal to his white working-class and middle-class constituents was based on his conservative, law-and-order image. But surely if we look beyond his image to the policies enacted by his administration, we would not label as "conservative" an investment program that disproportionately benefited poor black neighborhoods.


## CONCLUSION


In the first chapter of this volume, I reviewed three models of the municipal decision-making process that are commonly used to explain the low levels of public investment in the city's poor neighborhoods. The data I have presented in this chapter lead me to conclude that the assumption made by all three models regarding public disinvestment from the inner city must be seriously qualified to be useful in explaining the patterns of capital spending for community facilities. The pluralist model posits that an administration's capital investments directly reflect its political obligations; physical facilities are dispensed, like jobs and favors, to pay political debts. I have argued, however, that such a direct relationship between political support and public investments was difficult to detect in the 1960s and altogether missing in the 1970s. That capital spending need not follow the contours of the political map is obvious from the analysis of the investments made under Mayor Rizzo in the 1970s. From the perspective of political economy, municipal decision makers would have been expected to withdraw investments from inner city areas as their populations became increasingly marginal to the production process. Economic and governmental elites would be expected to direct the city's investment in social overhead capital to neighborhoods containing its productive population. And yet the inner city appeared to draw a greater share of investments as its marginality increased. Nor does the "triage" model of decision making apply without modification to my data, since the proportion of the total investment in community facilities in the most blighted areas actually increased from 1950 to 1970.

Explaining the patterns of distribution among the city's neighborhoods in the postwar years is increasingly a matter of tracking the priorities and strategies of municipal bureaucrats and planners, as influenced by federal policies. Through the elitist reform of the 1950s and the turbulent 1960s, there is some evidence of political influences outside the bureaucracy, although the major influence on the plan was that of planners and redevelopment officials. But by the 1970s, bureaucratic dominance had increased dramatically. More projects were included in the annual capital plan than could possibly be built, and thus city administrators began taking increasing responsibility for making those choices long after both planners and elected politicians had played their respective roles. Even the city council's strong assertion of its prerogatives in the early 1980s (about which I will say more in chapter 5) does not appear likely to change this situation, because of the council's practice of overcommitting funds and then leaving it to the finance director and department heads to decide which of the many projects actually get built.

To accept this interpretation of bureaucratic primacy in the allocation process is not necessarily to assume that community residents' demands make no difference to the system. In fact, on those occasions when residents have mobilized either in favor or in opposition to particular projects, they have often prevailed. But as Bryan Jones has pointed out, the fact of a favorable decision does not necessarily prove that citizen demands *forced* the response. Jones' analysis in Detroit suggests that citizen demands for service are often treated by municipal bureaucrats as information about needs existing in the environment; collecting citizen complaints or demands is part of the bureaucrats' intelligence-gathering and treated as one element of the calculation about where to deploy their resources. Jones rejects "the demand-response explanation of neighborhoods forcing bureaucracies to deliver services," asserting instead that [citizen] inputs are purely informational, part of a decision rule which dictates where organizational resources are to go."[17]

To sum up, my analysis suggests that during the 1960s and 1970s bureaucratic decision rules became increasingly important determinants of allocation decisions by the municipality. A decision rule that stressed a wider dispersal of investments led to more generous allocations to poor areas in the 1960s; a decision framework dominated by austerity conditions in the 1970s led to a worst-first pattern. In one sense this is not surprising, since a number of other studies have come to a similar conclusion regarding the importance of bureaucratic routines. But virtually all of those earlier studies focused on *operating* budgets as opposed to *capital* budgets, and a convincing case can be made that the two budgetary processes are characterized by different kinds of issues, different kinds of politics, and different kinds of decision making. So striking are these differences that they have prompted some analysts to question whether bureaucratic decision rules actually have any significant impact on capital expenditures.[18] Capital projects have traditionally been perceived as far more susceptible to political manipulation than operating budgets; indeed, buying support with pork-barrel expenditures is a time-honored political tradition. Yet the Philadelphia experience challenges the interpretation of municipal facilities as invariably a pork-barrel enterprise, showing that at certain periods municipal bureaucrats may play the dominant role in deciding who gets what, when and where.

4

# Community Facilities and Neighborhood Housing Markets

I N estimating the contribution made by community facilities to neighborhood development, city planners in Philadelphia as elsewhere have operated largely on the basis of intuition and professional judgments, rather than on empirical evidence. The assumption that community facilities can support and encourage residential development or redevelopment lay behind a good deal of the planning done under urban renewal programs of the 1950s and 1960s, as well as more recent planning efforts within the Community Development Block Grant Program. And yet the empirical evidence for this belief is virtually nonexistent.

## THE RELATIONSHIP OF COMMUNITY IMPROVEMENTS TO HOUSING VALUES

Granted, opinion surveys have consistently pointed to the importance of the neighborhood environment, including its physical attributes, as

81

a crucial determinant of residential satisfaction. For example, a 1971 study by the University of Michigan Survey Research Center demonstrated that neighborhood attributes (specifically, public schools, climate, streets and roads, parks and playgrounds, police-community relations, and local taxes) were more important than either the size of the community or the characteristics of the individual household in predicting residential satisfaction.[1] A 1982 study confirmed that the quality of the neighborhood environment (measured by its public schools, access to outdoor areas, safety, recreational facilities, and transportation) was the strongest variable accounting for residential satisfaction.[2] Extrapolating from such attitudinal findings, numerous economists have theorized about the effects on property values of municipal services[3] and physical improvements.[4] Such economic analyses draw their basic assumption from an observation made by turn-of-the-century Progressives like Henry George and Frederic Howe that tax dollars spent by local governments on public improvements and services add significantly to the value of private property. (Henry George is of course best known for his proposal that local governments should structure property taxes in ways that capture for the public treasury some of the value added to private property by various kinds of tax-supported public works.) Observers of urban land markets have traditionally reasoned that the value of a plot depends directly on its proximity to jobs, stores, churches, and a host of publicly provided services. As Gideon Sjoberg put it, "the highly valued residence is where fullest advantage may be taken of the city's strategic facilities."[5]

Charles Tiebout theorized in 1956 that the levels and types of expenditures made by a local government would influence the demand for residential property within that municipality. Tiebout envisioned a kind of open competition among the various municipalities located within a metropolitan region, each one offering a unique combination of services and tax burdens. In this model, metropolitan residents act as consumers of public services, selecting the particular package of burdens and benefits that best satisfies their preferences.[6] Like Tiebout, the economists who followed have relied on a household utility maximization model to explore the probable effects of different kinds of public expenditures and improvements, assuming that these expenditures increase the demand for property in the area, thereby increasing housing values. Most of the theoretical literature on this subject to date has used the metropolitan region as its hypothetical arena, and has assumed a high enough level of mobility to permit residents to express their preferences by moving from one jurisdiction to another.

The general conclusion reached by these theorists is that municipal services and improvements, especially school improvements, can be expected to have a positive effect on housing values. But whether conclusions reached under these assumptions can be applied to a single aging industrial city with a sizable population of poor and minority residents is questionable. The level of mobility enjoyed by much of Philadelphia's population is far below the ideal level hypothesized in most of these models.

If we turn from economic theory to empirical research, we find only a small number of studies that have actually tried to measure the impact of municipal policies on property values,[7] and most of those that do exist have focused on operating expenditures as a way to operationalize municipal policy outputs. Wallace Oates first estimated the effects of public school expenditures and property taxes on housing values in fifty-three New Jersey communities.[8] His work was followed by other studies which looked at other types of municipal expenditures in other parts of the country,[9] usually examining the effects of both property taxes and public spending at the same time. Because of the direct link between operating budgets and property taxes in most American cities, increases in services are invariably associated with increases in tax rates, with the two changes having opposing effects on housing values. One recent study of eleven central cities and eighty-nine suburban communities concluded that the gain in investments in these communities that resulted from improved services was almost exactly equal to the loss they suffered from raising property taxes. Their net gain, in terms of attracting residential investment, was zero.[10] But these conclusions drawn from empirical research focusing on municipal operating expenditures cannot be automatically applied to the issue of the benefits generated by capital projects. For one thing, capital projects are financed by long-term debt, rather than through the annual operating budget, and therefore the cost burden is not so immediately felt by property-owning taxpayers. Moreover, the benefits of a particular capital improvement are often localized, whereas its cost is spread out across all municipal taxpayers. Thus it is conceivable that a neighborhood that gets a new school or library would realize a net gain in property values, simply because the neighborhood would reap virtually all the benefit while shifting some of the cost to the rest of the city.

Unfortunately, there is almost no empirical evidence on the influence that community facilities have on property values in neighborhoods where they are located. Under a contract with the Department of Housing and Urban Development, the American Society of Planning Officials in 1977 prepared a synopsis of the research available on the role of capital improvements in community development. After reviewing the existing research on the impact of utility systems, highways, and public transportation on residential development, the authors turned to the subject of community facilities. Their findings are worth quoting at length:

> Although the design, construction, and operation of such facilities (as schools, libraries, police and fire stations, recreation and health centers) are common to most general-purpose local governments, there is little solid evidence in the literature empirically describing their influence on community development patterns. . . . The issue of whether such facilities precede and may help induce development or reinvestment or support development is particularly difficult to determine. In many large-scale projects, in both cities and developing areas, private and public investment occur more or less concurrently. Questions of "impact" here seldom are raised, except intuitively. There are many proposals for development, redevelopment, or stabilization of cities or parts of cities, but these offer little or no empirical data. The voluminous community facilities planning literature also failed to yield much evidence of actual impacts.[11]

Yet the absence of empirical evidence on the subject has certainly not prevented planners from trying to use capital improvements to shape community development. In 1941 Edmund Bacon, who was not yet executive director of the City Planning Commission, made a forceful statement before the Philadelphia Real Estate Board, expressing his conviction that public facilities must be built in order to bolster neighborhood housing markets. The lack of such elementary facilities as playgrounds and parks, he asserted, was accelerating neighborhood decline in some parts of the city, because families were moving to the suburbs to enjoy these basic amenities. (Bacon's views, in a limited sense, presaged the Tiebout theory of residential consumerism.) On the basis of his belief he concluded:

> The expenditure of some public funds for this purpose would be a good investment, as it would tend to stabilize the value of property which is, after all, the primary source of municipal revenue.[12]

Bacon's views were echoed fifteen years later by the head planner for the Redevelopment Authority, in a massive evaluation of the results of Philadelphia's urban renewal program. The 1956 report, known as the Central Urban Renewal Area (CURA) study, complained that the city's policy of targeting urban renewal projects to its most blighted sections was simply untenable, given the limited resources available for redevelopment. This worst-first strategy created small islands of renewal which were soon overwhelmed by the surrounding blight. Instead, the CURA study recommended shifting resources away from the most deteriorated parts of the inner city, to neighborhoods where decay was less advanced and where some public investment might turn the situation around. A key recommendation for the treatment of these not-so-poor neighborhoods was the provision of community facilities in order to stabilize the housing markets and prevent further decline.[13] Although the study recommendations were never fully implemented, they did reaffirm the view that public investments in community facilities could be used to leverage private residential investment.

This view surfaced once again in the 1960 Comprehensive Plan. Describing the total costs and revenue sources, the plan's framers asserted that "this public investment will stimulate private investment many times as great."[14] Their intent was to improve the quality of life within the city in order to permit Philadelphia's neighborhoods to compete successfully with suburban residential environments.[15] The capacity of public investments to leverage private resources became a major theme in the work of the city administrators who were charged with implementing the plan. As I explained earlier, in chapter 2, the plan identified the capital improvements that should be undertaken over the succeeding twenty years, but it did not set any priorities for building them. City administrators were therefore faced with the task of deciding which departmental requests for capital projects should be honored first. In this regard, the city economist Kirk Petshek played a key role.

To help establish such priorities, one device he used was the elite opinion survey described in chapter 2 to gain some sense of the priorities held by the civic establishment. Another approach (first recommended by Petshek and later endorsed by the managing director and finance director) was to require each department, when submitting its capital requests, to justify the priority being given to individual projects, using criteria such as the need for the project and the fit between this and other projects of the department, as well as conformity with the Comprehensive Plan. Petshek insisted that these departmental justifications for projects address their neighborhood economic impacts:

> The first problem is obviously how property values in the area of the project will be affected. This is particularly important in the case of redevelopment, where, in a way, the improvement of the whole area is part of the basic idea. . . . The second problem is how private investment is likely to be affected by the capital program. Ideally any public works should make the area more desirable and therefore stimulate private capital expenditures.[16]

The data I have collected on capital expenditures for community facilities in 104 Philadelphia neighborhoods should be useful in determining whether the hopes of these early postwar planners have been justified. Can we, in retrospect, detect any positive contribution made by community facilities to neighborhood housing markets? If we can, the next question must be how important that influence is, relative to the other influences shaping urban neighborhoods.

## EVIDENCE FROM THE PHILADELPHIA CASE

To tackle this question, we need some measure of the condition of neighborhood housing markets that we can track across the thirty-year period for which we have expenditure data. The measure I have chosen is the median value of owner-occupied housing units as reported in the census, which seemed the best single indicator of market trends in any given neighborhood:[17] Housing values have changed rapidly in some parts of the city, producing contrasts between declining and gentrifying areas that lie side by side. Some appreciation of how dramatic those contrasts have been can be gained from table 4.1, which gives housing values for the same four neighborhoods that were depicted in figure 3.1 of the last chapter. The reader will remember that these four neighborhoods lie adjacent to one another, just north of the central business district. The numbers in table 4.1 show that all four neighborhoods had housing values below the citywide average up to 1970. But at that point two of them, Fairmount and Spring Garden, underwent a process of gentrification that produced dramatic increases in their respective housing markets. The housing market in the Poplar neighborhood made slight gains during the 1970s, which left

**Table 4.1**

Median Value of Owner-Occupied Units in Four Philadelphia Neighborhoods, 1950 to 1980

|  | *1950* | *1960* | *1970* | *1980* |
|---|---|---|---|---|
| Fairmount | $4,923 | $6,737 | $7,167 | $34,694 |
| Spring Garden | 5,188 | 7,616 | 8,257 | 63,342 |
| Cabot | 4,617 | 6,536 | 4,735 | 9,998 |
| Poplar | 4,415 | 5,752 | 9,716 | 22,648 |
| Citywide | 7,720 | 8,700 | 10,712 | 23,700 |

it still below the citywide average, while the fourth area, Cabot, remained one of the weakest housing markets in the city in 1980.

Having charted the changes in housing market conditions across the city, we now turn to the question of whether those changes were related to public investments in community facilities. Our first step is to see what association exists between: (1) the expenditures made in the postwar period for community facilities, and (2) the changes in housing values. Table 4.2 presents zero-order correlations of per capita spending for both schools and city-owned facilities (libraries, recreation facilities, police and fire stations), with changes in housing values. The reader should observe that in the tables that follow, spending is being correlated, not with the absolute value of owner-occupied houses in any given year, but rather with the *change* in housing values during the period in which the spending took place. So, for example, we are asking whether the amount of money invested between 1950 and 1959 in neighborhood facilities was associated with a proportional increase in house value between 1950 and 1960. In table 4.2 the only coefficient that is significant at the .01 level is that for school spending in the 1970s. Yet surprisingly the coefficient carries a negative sign, as do four other coefficients, all too small to be significant. Because the results are inconclusive, we cannot necessarily infer that increased expenditures per acre are associated with housing decline. But at a

**Table 4.2**

Correlations of Spending on Community Facilities with Change in Housing Values

|  | *1950s* | *1960s* | *1970s* |
|---|---|---|---|
| Schools | −.029 | −.049 | −.241* |
| City facilities | +.004 | −.065 | −.154 |

*Significant at the .01 level

minimum, the figures challenge the idea that there is a direct positive relationship between spending and housing improvement.

These findings are especially surprising with respect to school spending, because previous studies that have looked at the impact of municipal operating expenditures on housing values have generally concluded that school expenditures *are* associated with rising housing values. One possible explanation for this discrepancy might be the extraordinary popularity of private schools in Philadelphia. Nearly one-third of the city's school children now attend nonpublic schools, and some estimates put the figure even higher for earlier decades. (For example, the United States Commission on Civil Rights estimated in 1962 that Catholic schools alone accounted for 38% of all Philadelphia schoolchildren.)[18] The public school system ends up serving families who cannot afford private schools and, as a result, has perhaps invested a larger share of its resources in declining areas of the city than has the city government. We might hypothesize that in these declining areas, the housing market was too weak to respond positively to new investment.

One way to test this hypothesis is to run the correlation analysis again, but this time to exclude from the analysis any neighborhoods whose housing markets might be considered too weak to respond to new facilities investments. The results of that analysis are presented in table 4.3 For each decade, I excluded from the analysis the twenty neighborhoods having the lowest median house values at the start of the decade. The consequence, as can be seen, was not to strengthen the association between spending and changing housing values. Again, only one coefficient emerged as significant. How do we explain the fact that we see no stronger correlation, even after excluding the weakest neighborhood housing markets? One possible explanation for the disappointing results is that funds were not sufficiently "targeted," or concentrated in specific geographical areas.

**Table 4.3**

Correlations of Spending on Community Facilities with Change in Housing Values, Excluding Neighborhoods with the Weakest Housing Markets

|  | 1950s | 1960s | 1970s |
|---|---|---|---|
| Schools | −.068 | −.020 | −.226* |
| City facilities | +.013 | −.017 | −.157 |

*Significant at the .05 level

Since the 1950s regional economists have held the view that in order to promote development in lagging regions, governments must make a large enough investment to create a self-sustaining growth center. This view is based upon the observations that economic and social development occur unevenly in geographical space, and that once development appears in an area, powerful forces operating in the private sector economy will promote further concentration of development in that same location. Thus, economists have advised policy makers to use their limited resources to assist locales in reaching the "take-off" point, after which they would be propelled by market forces.[19] They can do so, in the view of many economists, by creating *in advance* of development the very kinds of amenities that would normally *follow* growth. That is, demands for well-developed transportation networks, sewage systems, schools, hospitals, and even cultural facilities are the kinds of infrastructure demands that one would expect to result from residential development (or redevelopment). By providing that infrastructure in advance, it is hoped governments can attract new capital to designated growth centers. Because the essential consideration in carrying out such a development scheme is to invest sufficient public money in a single location to achieve take-off, the key to success lies in targeting infrastructure investments to a few locales rather than dispensing resources too widely.

While they originated in the regional development literature, these notions of uneven development, "hot spots," and investment thresholds were picked up quickly by those concerned with inner city renewal as well. The federal Model Cities program, for example, required cities to designate specific poverty areas of limited size for a combination of physical investments and social service activities: "HUD would channel the existing flow of federal resources from other agencies into selected poverty neighborhoods where a great concentration of effort could demonstrate significant results."[20]

Although the Community Development Block Grant program, which replaced urban renewal and Model Cities in 1974, gave local officials more freedom to designate development areas as they saw fit, the legislation nevertheless contained provisions that assumed local governments would continue to target their efforts. For example, the legislation permitted cities to use Community Development funds for public facilities, so long as those facilities were located in or served "designated community development areas." Similarly, cities could use funds for social services only if they were part of a larger set of community development activities concentrated in particular areas.

"The overall effect of these provisions was to make program concentration an underlying, if not explicit, characteristic of the block grant."[21]

Having noted the general consensus among economists and planners that investment is likely to produce positive changes in an area only if sufficiently concentrated, let us return to our expenditure data to see just how concentrated the investment in community facilities has been. In constructing figure 4.1, I identified for each decade the twenty-one neighborhoods (approximately 20% of all the neighborhoods) in which the city invested the largest dollar amounts. I went through the same procedure for the school district. The object was to see just what proportion of the total expenditures in each decade had been concentrated in these favored areas. The figure shows a fair degree of concentration, particularly in the 1970s when the city spent fully two-thirds of its money in areas containing less than a quarter of the city's total land area and only 19% of its population. The school district pattern is even more highly concentrated, because each individual school building is so expensive to build that the total cannot be spread over very many areas.

But having established that there has been some degree of concentration in investment patterns, especially in the 1970s, can we also show that concentration produced greater benefits for the neighborhoods where the investment surpassed a minimum threshold? Table 4.4 presents a revised correlation analysis using only neighborhoods where the combined investment by the city and school district exceeded $25 per person. (This criterion eliminated 52 neighborhoods in the 1950s, 36 in the 1960s, and 58 in the 1970s.) My purpose is to test for a threshold effect—that is, to see whether stronger correlations between public investment and housing improvements can be detected in this sample than were obtained when we included all 104 neighborhoods. It is obvious from table 4.4 that confining the analysis only to areas that passed a certain spending threshold makes little difference in the outcome. Not a single significant association emerges from the data. Moreover, as many of the signs are positive as negative. By now, we are tempted to accept the possibility that investment in community facilities is simply not associated with housing values. And yet there is still another way to approach the question that might yield a different result.

Thus far, we have been exploring the bivariate relationship between facilities spending and housing change, with disappointing results. However, a multitude of other forces operate in neighborhood

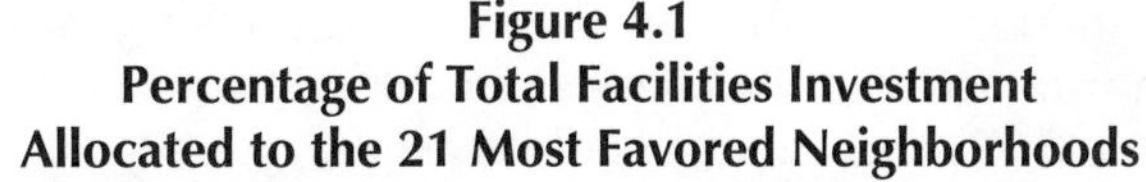

**Figure 4.1**
**Percentage of Total Facilities Investment**
**Allocated to the 21 Most Favored Neighborhoods**

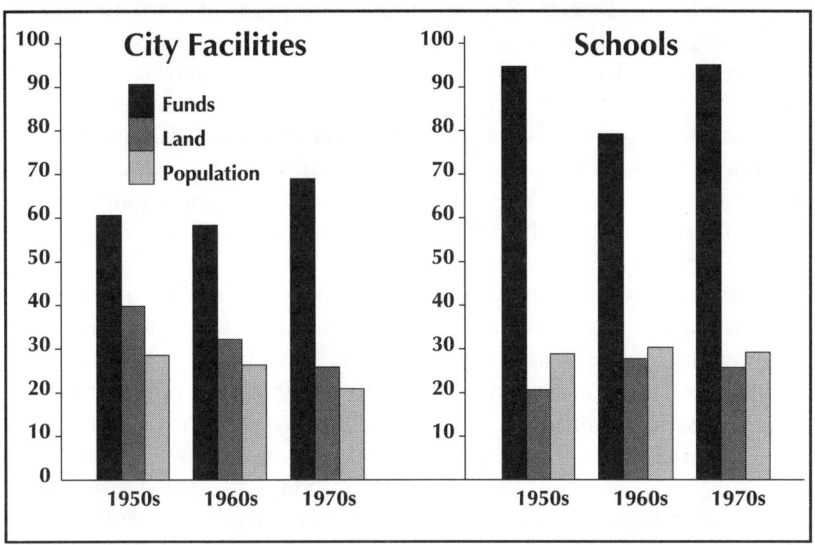



housing markets, any of which might be distorting, or even masking altogether, the relationship we are seeking to establish between public investment and neighborhood change. One way to examine this possibility is to employ multiple regression analysis, a statistical technique that allows us to observe the relationship between two variables while controlling the influence of other factors. In other words, the technique allows us to see whether, other things being equal, there exists a relationship between our two key variables. To do so requires us first to identify the other important forces that may account for changes in neighborhood housing markets. I have chosen to include in the analysis four of the factors that are most commonly cited as determinants

**Table 4.4**

Correlations of Spending on Community Facilities with Change in Housing Values, Excluding Neighborhoods Receiving Less Than $25 Per Capita

|                | *1950s* | *1960s* | *1970s* |
|----------------|---------|---------|---------|
| Schools        | +.080   | −.061   | −.193   |
| City facilities | +.224   | −.039   | +.039   |

of housing market strength, and therefore of housing values. Once again, I am interested in the changes in these factors over time, and the extent to which such changes affect neighborhood housing.

The first of these factors is simply change in the absolute size of the population, included on the grounds that an expanding population suggests increasing demand for housing in a particular area, while a shrinking population means that demand is likely to soften. At the extreme, of course, the exodus of large numbers of residents from a neighborhood can lead to abandonment and a precipitous drop in neighborhood viability. We would therefore expect population change to be a factor influencing the strength of submarkets and, consequently, housing values.

A second determinant of vitality that is often cited in the real estate literature as well as in sociological models of neighborhood life cycles is the age of the housing stock. Ever since Homer Hoyt asserted in 1939 that "there is a constant outward movement of neighborhoods because as neighborhoods become older they tend to be less desirable," planners have believed that housing loses value as it ages. Consequently, we would expect neighborhoods with substantial new construction to have greater appeal than older areas. I have therefore included an indicator of the age of neighborhood housing stock. My measure is the percentage of units over twenty years old, and the change variable included in the equation is the change in that percentage from one census to another. We anticipate that this variable will be negatively related to housing values; increases in the proportion of older housing should produce lower housing values.

The third and fourth factors are race and income of the neighborhood's residents, both factors that have been identified in countless studies as contributors to neighborhood change. The variables included in the equation are the change in the percentage of nonwhite residents and the change in the median household income. Housing values are expected to be negatively associated with the former, and positively associated with the latter.

Table 4.5 displays the standardized regression coefficients, or "beta weights," for the five independent variables expected to predict neighborhood housing vitality. The advantage of this measure over the unstandardized regression coefficient is that it portrays the relationships among variables after their raw values have been converted into standard deviation units. Because the units of measure are comparable for all of the variables, we can compare the coefficients to one another, in order to assess the relative strength of the different independent variables as predictors of the dependent variable.

Of our five independent variables, only two prove to be significant and carry the expected sign: change in the percent nonwhite and change in the median income. Surprisingly, the change in the size of the population as a whole shows only a weak association with housing vitality, and the relationship is inverse. That means that at least for some neighborhoods in Philadelphia, increases in the housing values between 1950 and 1979 were associated with population losses. This finding is reminiscent of an argument made by Jane Jacobs in the early 1960s that population declines are often found in neighborhoods that are in the process of "unslumming," because of a shrinkage in the average household size. In making this observation, Jacobs was referring to neighborhoods in which the economic circumstances of long-time residents have gradually improved:

> Paradoxically, this (population drop) is a signal of popularity. It means that formerly overcrowded inhabitants who have become economically able to uncrowd are doing so in their old neighborhood instead of abandoning it to a new wave of the overcrowded.[22]

However, it is equally true that some neighborhoods experience a population decline in the process of gentrifying, because the incoming households have higher incomes and living standards than the residents whom they displace. We might therefore speculate that it is the

**Table 4.5**

Beta Weights for Change in Housing Values, 1950–1979, and Selected Independent Variables

| | |
|---|---|
| Change in size of population, 1959–1979 | −.046 |
| Change in % older housing, 1950–1979 | −.103 |
| Change in percent nonwhite, 1950–1979 | −.229* |
| Change in median income, 1950–1979 | +.649* |
| Facilities expenditures, 1950–1979 | +.003 |

$R^2$ = .526
F  = 21.8
*Significant at the .01 level.

connection between neighborhood upgrading and smaller household size that has distorted the expected link between population change and the housing values.

Nor is the change in the proportion of older housing a good predictor of changes in the housing submarkets of Philadelphia, probably because some older areas of the city have gained in popularity in the postwar period. As expected, change in the percent nonwhite is found to be inversely related to neighborhood housing conditions; increases in the number of nonwhite residents are associated with declines in house values. However, the most striking feature of table 4.6 is the overwhelming importance of changes in median income in predicting changes in the housing values. Rising incomes are strongly associated with improving housing markets. That finding in itself is not surprising, but what is unexpected is the extent to which it dominates the equation. Taken together, these five independent variables account for 53% of the variation in the dependent variable, and obviously the equation's explanatory power lies overwhelmingly in the income variable. Compared to racial change in neighborhoods, income change is a far better predictor of the direction of the housing market.

Unfortunately, the equation also demonstrates that even after we have controlled for the effects of both income and racial change, there is still no detectable impact of facilities investments on neighborhood housing conditions. It now seems reasonable to conclude that no such relationships exists.


## THE MISSING CONNECTION BETWEEN COMMUNITY IMPROVEMENTS AND HOUSING VALUES

How can we explain the failure to demonstrate any relationship between community improvements and housing values in neighborhoods across Philadelphia? The data simply do not confirm the planners' assumption that they could bolster housing markets and influence residential choices by the placement of modern public facilities. There are a number of possible explanations for this disappointing finding. I will present them in turn, though unfortunately the data do not allow me to choose among them.

The model I have been testing in this study is one based on market forces. The built-in assumption has been that different neighborhoods have different attributes (including presence of community facilities) whose relative desirability or undesirability will be reflected in differential house values. At least since Tiebout, researchers have analyzed residential mobility in cities as a matter of the households' consumption of the benefits and costs associated with a particular location, and planners have assumed that parks, schools, and libraries furnish significant consumption benefits to nearby residents. My findings might be interpreted to mean that, contrary to conventional wisdom, residents derive few consumptions benefits from the presence of new or expanded public facilities within their neighborhood, and hence such facilities contribute little to the attractiveness of housing markets. A corollary would be that the lack of new investments in facilities is not a sufficient drawback to encourage current residents to leave the neighborhood.

This possibility, while it runs counter to the expectations of many planners, would be consistent with the findings of a study done almost thirty years ago in Philadelphia by Peter Rossi. He interviewed over nine hundred households in four areas of the city (Oak Lane, West Philadelphia, Kensington, and Center City) in order to ascertain what factors led people to move to new locations. Surprisingly, he found that the complaints they expressed about the proximity of their present housing to jobs, stores, and facilities (including schools) were not very good predictors of actual moves. Such complaints were far less powerful predictors of mobility than were complaints about the present dwelling unit (space, heating, closets, etc.) and the social characteristics of the neighborhood.[23] Rossi's findings suggest that the presence of schools, libraries, and recreation centers nearby may simply not be an important factor influencing housing choices. Similar conclusions emerged from a recent national study of sixty thousand households living in metropolitan areas across the country. The data for the study came from interviews contained in the Census Bureau's Annual Housing Survey, and its purpose was to analyze the major motives influencing a household's decision to move. The researchers concluded that " concerns about public services did not play a meaningful role in explaining variations in mobility," and thus that "efforts to hold existing residents of declining areas through improved services have relatively little potential for success."[24]

Yet another possible explanation for my finding is that the presence of nearby facilities *is* an attractive feature of neighborhoods, but that their benefits must be weighed against certain costs generated by those same facilities. After all, increases in noise, pollution, traffic, and the presence of large numbers of youths congregated around schools and recreation centers are all likely to result from the addition or expansion of community facilities. It may be that these costs associated with facilities have a negative impact which offsets their consumption benefits, thereby eliminating any *net* positive effect. While some work has been done on negative perceptions of public facilities, the work so far has concentrated primarily on residential opposition to noxious facilities such as highways, certain types of urban renewal projects, projects involving high-risk technologies and projects that attract so-called undesirables to the neighborhood (for example, drug/alcohol rehabilitation clinics, halfway houses, etc.) Facilities such as these are perceived as reducing the desirability of the surrounding community, and it is hardly surprising that community activists resist them.[25]

There are also cases in which neighborhood residents oppose a public facility that could not be classified as "noxious," and yet may be unwanted. For example, one member of the Philadelphia City Council was surprised to discover that an ice-skating rink for his district in West Philadelphia, which he had fought to have included in the 1982–83 capital budget, was actually opposed by a very vocal group of his constituents. About two hundred elderly people living near the proposed site for the rink organized themselves as the Cobbs Creek Area Concerned Citizens to defeat the plan because they believed it would attract large numbers of youths in the evenings, and thereby increase vandalism in their neighborhood. The rink has never been constructed, and while its delay must be attributed to a number of factors, it surely did not help the project to have an organized group of community residents opposing it.

Alternatively we might speculate that the problem lies in our assumption that the housing market efficiently translates a neighborhood's consumption benefits into housing prices. This assumption requires that Philadelphia residents express their preferences by moving and bidding up the prices in neighborhoods that satisfy those preferences. As we noted early in this chapter, the market model has produced some positive results when applied to suburban housing markets; that is, some researchers have found that the level of spending on services by suburban governments does indeed translate into higher housing values in the community. And yet, our findings in Philadelphia lead us to question whether the assumption of household utility maximization holds for the city's housing market. Both the ability and the willingness of central city dwellers to move, in order to take advantage of a better location elsewhere, are lower than for suburban households.[26] The Philadelphia housing market is highly segmented, by race, ethnicity, and income level, and this segmentation reduces the housing options for long-term residents.[27] Support for this hypothesis is provided by the national study cited above, which was based on sixty thousand households drawn from the Annual Housing Survey. That research showed that blacks are far less likely to move than whites, even when they express dissatisfaction with their present housing and neighborhood.[28]

The market's failure to translate all consumer preferences into effective demand for housing is not only hampered by the compartmentalization of urban housing markets, but also by the fact that so many urban dwellers have too little income to exercise their preferences. The utility of nearby public facilities is likely to be highest for low-income residents because they have fewer private-market alternatives (like private schools, swim clubs, tennis clubs, etc.). Yet they are the least able to translate their preferences into effective demand for housing locations that are well-served by public facilities. At the same time more affluent residents who have greater ability to "buy" proximity to community facilities, are less likely to regard the presence of such facilities as a crucial factor in making a housing choice. Thus, the presence of modern public facilities in the neighborhood may provide genuine consumption benefits even though those benefits are not reflected in higher housing prices.

A neo-Marxist interpretation of my findings would challenge the idea of consumer sovereignty that is built into the market model. As I noted in chapter, 1, the neo-Marxists see housing supply and housing prices as a function of the availability of capital rather than as a reflection of consumer demand for housing. On that view, one would not necessarily expect to see housing prices move in accordance with the consumption benefits that the dwellings provide. Put in the vocabulary of neo-Marxists, a property's "use value" (for its residents) need not coincide with its "exchange value" (for the marketplace).[29] A new park or neighborhood swimming pool may well bring higher consumption benefits to an area, but that fact will not automatically be reflected in higher housing prices. Instead, investor decisions hold the key to price changes. Even massive public investment in a neighborhood will not stimulate housing prices if lending institutions do not supply mortgage capital. And public policies that try to enhance the attractiveness of neighborhoods to consumers (for example, by proving community improvements) will be less successful than policies that appeal directly to investors.

In rapidly growing suburbs the most attractive investment opportunities coincide with the most desirable consumption opportunities. Those communities that provide the best services and amenities are also likely to represent ideal investment environments for banks, developers, and other suppliers of capital. In such places the provision of community facilities is associated with rising housing values. Hence, the frequent finding by researchers that suburban spending for schools, parks, libraries, etc., *is* in fact correlated with improving property values. But in declining or even stable areas the relationship does not hold. This is probably because investors do not perceive the presence of community facilities as contributing to securing their investment, regardless of the consumption benefits provided for residents.

## CONCLUSION

Despite the expectations of economists and planners alike that investment in community facilities can be used to strengthen housing submarkets, I have been unable to confirm that expectation with my data. According to this analysis, city and school district expenditures on neighborhood facilities over a thirty-year period had an insignificant impact on housing market conditions, as measured by the median value of owner-occupied housing. The overwhelmingly important factor in accounting for changes in housing values was the change in the income of residents—a factor over which city planners have virtually no control.

My findings call into question the utility of traditional market models in analyzing inner city housing markets. To expect property values to mirror the consumption benefits available in various neighborhoods, we must assume the market is effectively translating housing preferences into prices. We must also assume housing prices are determined primarily by consumer preferences. Neither assumption may be justified. Poor people often cannot express their preferences through purchasing power. As cities like Philadelphia have gained larger concentrations of poor, their housing markets are less and less likely to reflect the true preferences of residents. It may also be the case, as neo-Marxists have argued, that consumer preferences do not drive neighborhood change anyway; investor behavior does.

Nor do my findings support the general assumption in much of the literature on public capital investments that there *is* a relationship between public and private investment patterns. Admittedly, researchers have made little progress in specifying precisely what that relationship is. Many studies, as I have already noted, assume that public investment precedes and encourages private development. That is the assumption behind Philadelphia's *1960 Comprehensive Plan* and most of the urban renewal efforts since World War II. Equally common, it appears, is the assumption that public facilities and programs follow private investment patterns because an influx of private residential development increases the demand for public services as well as furnishing the tax base to support such services.[30] Whether one subscribes to the lead or lag theory or both (that is, circular relationship), few researchers have expressed any doubt that levels of public and private investments will covary.

My data on social overhead capital in Philadelphia, however, show that public investments in schools, recreation, libraries, and police and fire stations neither lead nor lag private investment in housing. Indeed, public and private investment do not seem to be related at all. City officials who allocate tax dollars for community facilities have apparently based their decisions on other criteria than residential investment patterns.

Taken together, this chapter and the last can be read as a "good news/bad news" report. The good news, outlined in the last chapter, is that low-income and minority neighborhoods shared equally, even disproportionately, in public investments made in community facilities between 1950 and 1979. The bad news is, of course, that those investments had no observable impact on neighborhood housing conditions. Neither in the poorer sections of the city nor in the more affluent ones could I attribute housing changes to the presence or absence of such investment.

The absence of a demonstrable link between these two does *not* mean that the distribution of neighborhood facilities is unimportant. As the next chapter will show, decisions about the placement of playgrounds and swimming pools often carry tremendous symbolic importance. The analysis in this chapter simply shows that the relationship between government outputs (in the form of facilities built) and neighborhood outcomes is not so direct as some planners and policy makers have expected it to be.

# 5

# Political Struggles over Cutbacks and Closures

T HE rediscovery in the 1980s of the urban infrastructure as a major problem for governments at all levels has focused almost entirely on the critical shortage of money being spent on construction, reconstruction, and maintenance of transportation, utility, and water/sewer systems. And yet, at the very same time that journalists, politicians, and economists are decrying the lack of investment in some types of urban infrastructure, they are beginning to talk about our cities' overcapitalization with respect to other types of infrastructure. The difference is that the first set of views invariably relates to what we described in the opening chapter as EOC, or economic overhead capital, whereas the second applies to SOC, or social overhead capital.

In a pure market economy, problems of overcapitalization or undercapitalization (relative to the profitability of investments) would be resolved by market forces. If the existing level of investment could not adequately serve the existing demand for a particular good or service, then new investors could be expected to move into the area to serve the surplus demand. Similarly, investors would respond to declining demand for their services or products by withdrawing capital. In the public sector, however, both the scale and location of investments in facilities are determined by public planners on grounds other than market competition.

In reality, of course, there are no "pure" markets operating solely on the basis of competitive conditions. Even in the private sector, investment decisions are based on many factors other than the market demand for a given product or service, one of which is the differential tax treatment afforded to different types of investment by local, state, and federal governments. Thus, George Sternlieb argued in the late 1970s that the United States was overcapitalized with respect to housing. The favorable tax treatment afforded to home buyers, combined with the rapid inflation in housing prices, Sternlieb reasoned, encouraged American families during the 1970s to devote a disproportionate share of income to housing, thereby reducing their ability to save and invest in the country's economic infrastructure. This willingness of consumers (as investors) to devote extraordinary shares of income to home ownership contributed to the economic stagnation and productivity problems experienced by the United States in the 1970s.[1]

Sternlieb's views about the overcapitalization of American housing in the 1970s are not unlike the views expressed by some observers about the overcapitalization of SOC in our cities. Their argument is that the allocation of too much of the nation's resources to cultural, recreational, educational, health, and welfare facilities drains investment away from more productive purposes. While in the long run such SOC investments may contribute to economic productivity by enhancing our "human capital," the benefits are indirect at best. In the short run, the economic revitalization of our cities demands that governments (1) limit taxation in order to leave more dollars in the private sector, and (2) invest the tax revenues they do obtain in more directly productive ways, to support and stimulate economic growth.

While these neoconservative ideas have found widespread acceptance among politicians and bureaucrats across the country, they are not the only motivation for the cutbacks in the support for community facilities now occurring in Philadelphia. Two much more immediate concerns are usually cited as the rationale for building fewer new facilities and closing some old ones. The first is the irrefutable fact that the population decline, which started in Philadelphia in 1950, has accelerated in recent years. After a decline of only 3% in the decades of the 1950s and 1960s, Philadelphia's population dropped another 13% in the 1970s. Since the need for SOC depends to some extent on the size of the population, this exodus can be expected to result in cuts in facilities. No one seriously believes that these cuts will be proportional to the numerical losses in population, given the composition of the remaining population. Because of the increasing concentration of elderly, poor, and minority groups in Philadelphia, as in other big cities, a larger proportion of the city's residents is dependent upon public services now than was previously the case. Furthermore, certain kinds of community facilities (e.g., fire stations) really provide services to households rather than to individual residents. And because of the constant shrinkage in average household size in recent decades, the massive population losses have produced only a slight drop in the number of households in the city. Hence, the 13% drop in the city's population between 1970 and 1979 did not necessarily mandate a 13% cut in community facilities.

The one category of facilities on which there seems to be general agreement that investment should follow population trends is public schools. Unlike the general population of the city, public school enrollments continued to increase in the 1950s and 1960s, peaking in 1970. But during the 1970s, the public school population shrank by over 50,000 pupils, and it is expected to drop by an additional 48,000 by 1990. Thus by 1990 the school district expects to be serving less than two-thirds the number of pupils it served in 1970.[2] There is little disagreement that population losses of this magnitude must be met by some school closings, although, as we shall see, attempts to move beyond that general observation to more specific recommendations have been exceedingly slow.

Besides population declines, which reduce the demand for community facilities, the other factor that is imposing restraint on the city's capital program is the burden new construction inevitably places on the city's operating budget. Because new facilities are generally financed by long-term debt rather than by current revenues, one might assume that the advent of tighter operating budgets in cities like Philadelphia would have only a negligible impact on the building program. Theodore Lowi, for instance, has speculated that because American cities are confronted with shrinking revenues, "the long-run bias of city activities and services will be toward public works and pension maintenance," the two major items that are not financed out of current budgets.[3] Lowi's generalization, however, needs to be qualified in order to distinguish between public works that are expected to generate additional tax revenues for the city, and those that are expected to place an additional burden on the annual operating budget. Most social overhead capital falls into the latter category. Even before opening day, each new library, recreation center, health center, etc., begins to draw on the operating budget for staff salaries and fringe benefits, supplies and equipment, lighting and heating, and for all of the expenses of day-to-day operation. During the 1970s the increasing sensitivity of some officials to these budgetary impacts of new construction led the city to try to curb the building program, especially of recreation facilities—a move we shall examine in greater detail later in the chapter.

Whether these budgetary and demographic shifts have the effect of limiting new construction projects or shutting down some existing facilities, conflict inevitably centers on which sites and which neighborhoods are involved. By its very definition, "capital programming" incites such conflict, because it entails the setting of priorities among various desirable public works projects and then the scheduling of construction (or alternatively, closures) on the basis of those priorities. The heart of the process thus lies in the priority setting. Who does this priority setting?

## SETTING PRIORITIES IN THE CAPITAL BUDGET

The 1951 city charter is quite explicit about the procedures to be followed in the preparation of the annual capital budget and the six- year capital program: requests for new projects are to be initiated within the operating departments, but then must be submitted to the City Planning Commission for review and for coordination with the city's Comprehensive Plan and with the plans of other departments. The charter appears to give the pivotal role to the Planning Commission, as adjudicator of the claims upon limited resources made by the various operating departments. Even the mayor, who receives the finished capital program from the Planning Commission, is not allowed to change the commission's document before passing it on to the city council; he may only append his recommendations for changes. The council itself, while it may freely eliminate projects, can only add new projects or change the dollar amounts after it has sought the Planning Commission's advice on such modifications. Finally, when the council's deliberations are completed and the capital program is sent back to the mayor, he is empowered to delete projects, but not to add to them. Hence, it is clear that the charter's framers wanted the commission to supply both the long-range, intersystem perspective that is so often lacking in the plans of individual operating departments, as well as the citywide viewpoint that is sometimes missing from the city council's deliberations.

How closely does this idealized statement of the commission's role accord with the actual postwar practice of capital programming? The answer to that question differs, depending upon the particular years in question, the types of facilities, and even the personalities involved. Two early commentators on the charter's capital planning provisions emphasized the latitude which that document provides, in accommodating different power configurations and different personalities:

> It (the charter) merely provided a multi-partitite decision, and left the actual distribution of influence to shifting developments in the channels of government, the tides of politics, and the shoals of personality.[4]

Two Planning Commission staff members, describing the early years' experience in implementing the new capital programming procedures outlined in the 1951 charter, acknowledged that their initial approach to dealing with the operating departments was to try to be cooperative and reasonable, gradually gaining authority and credibility.[5] After all, the city departments had been accustomed to bargaining directly with the city council, and could not be expected to greet the Planning Commission's new coordinating role with enthusiasm.

Typically, the mayor makes only minor and noncontroversial changes in the capital program prepared by the Planning Commission. But that is to be expected, given the commission's standard practice of widespread consultation and bargaining with the operating departments before the program is drawn up, and the presence of the mayor's three top-ranking cabinet officials as members of the commission. It is with the transmittal of the capital program to the city council that the priorities arrived at jointly by the commission and the city administration are open to serious challenge. Granted, the council is in the position of reacting to proposals that have been initiated by the operating departments, rather than trying to formulate its own capital program. And yet the power to delete projects, to change dollar allocations, and even to insert additional projects (after having solicited the opinion of the Planning Commission on the additions) gives the council the opportunity to alter significantly the priorities and choices expressed in the commission's program. In recent years the council has become more vocal in challenging the prepared document—a trend that appears to be directly related to the tightening budgets. As the fiscal squeeze has pushed the Planning Commission and the mayor's administration to make harder choices among projects, the council's dissatisfaction with those choices has grown. To illustrate the heightened political activity that now surrounds facilities planning, we will consider in turn two of the areas of greatest controversy: (1) the building of new recreation centers, and (2) the closing down of local public schools.


## RECREATION

The case of recreation is particularly instructive in displaying the potential for conflict that exists between the Planning Commission and the city council, based on the different sets of interests the two bodies represent. That potential has always existed; it was, in fact, built into the capital programming process by the charter. In commenting upon the different roles played by the Planning Commission and the council in the formation of capital budgets, staff planners at the commission in 1960 distinguished between their own "concerns for economy, functional efficiency, and aesthetics" and the council's obligation to represent "the needs and desires of the city's people."[6] Academic researchers studying Philadelphia's capital planning in 1960 put this distinction in more concrete terms. The council, they reported, had a shorter time frame than the Planning Commission and a more pronounced interest in health, welfare, and recreation facilities because those were of most immediate benefit to their constituents. The council's practice in the early postwar years, however, was to make changes in the Planning Commission's prepared capital program only with respect to scheduling projects. Rather than adding new projects or eliminating proposed projects, the council contented itself with moving individual expenditures forward or backward, or spreading them over longer time periods.[7] Hence, there were very few showdowns between the council and the commission in those early years.

Few observers of that period foresaw the strenuous, even acrimonious, disagreements over the capital program that would erupt among the council, the Planning Commission, and the mayor in the early 1980s. With the advantage of two decades' experience with the new charter, one of the veterans of Philadelphia's postwar planning analyzed the council's role as follows in 1973: The potential for conflict between the council on the one hand and the Planning Commission/mayor on the other hand, he reported, arises not simply from the council's shorter time frame and preference for certain types of projects. A more fundamental conflict of interests divides the legislative and executive branches of local government:

> The Council chamber became the backdrop against which the covert class warfare which is latent in all large cities was carried on. . . . The majority of the Council (especially after 1956) felt no kinship to the influential civic groups, whose members they saw . . . as representing only "big business," the financial fraternity, and the eggheads. . . . The Council felt the need to acknowledge that more had to be done for the "little man" who would (otherwise) be dispossessed.[8]

Kirk Petshek, the author of this trenchant comment on the city council's role in local politics, attributed its populist bent to the fact that the council had continued to be dominated by the regular Democratic party while the mayoral administration and Planning Commission were taken over by the reform Democrats. As he saw it, the conflict between executive and legislative branches was a conflict between opposing factions within the Democratic party. But the experience of more recent years suggests that a broader interpretation is needed. For in the late 1970s and early 1980s, the city council contained representatives of both the old-line Democratic regulars and the liberal reformist wing, as well as a number of powerful black politicians. Yet conflicts with the mayor and Planning Commission over the city's capital program have not necessarily developed along those factional lines. Instead, the tendency has been for council members from all factions of the Democratic and Republican parties to defend the council's prerogatives and positions against the administration.

The case of recreation planning nicely illustrates this point. From the viewpoint of constituency politics, recreation projects appear to be more important to council members than any other items in the capital budget. All council members, from the first-term freshmen to the veterans, watch carefully to see that their districts are taken care of and take pains to publicize their successes. Even the president of the council, a twelve-year incumbent in his district, publicly acknowledges his obligation to bring recreation dollars to his constituents. In his press release announcing that the 1983–84 capital budget contained $2 million for recreation improvements in his own district, Council President Coleman openly admitted, "One of my responsibilities as Councilman is to provide the money through City Council for requested capital improvements within my district. Once the money is in place, it is up to the neighborhoods and city departments to plan, develop, and ultimately complete the projects."[9]

So acutely do council members feel this obligation that even the council leadership is sometimes unable to cope with the resulting rivalries within the chamber. There have even been times when the council leadership was grateful for the intervention of the Planning Commission to resolve some disputes among the legislators. For example, Robert Mitchell recalled the following exchange between the commission and the council during his term as director of the Planning Commission in the 1940s:

> One day I had a call from the President of City Council, who said, "I have a problem. . . . All the city councilmen want recreation centers in their wards and we have quite a lot of sites proposed. What will I do with them . . . ? We can't afford it."
>
> So I said, "Well, send it over and I will put it up to our Recreation Advisory Committee,". . . and within a few days a report was sent back . . . .
>
> City Council took this report and acted upon it and in this way it had helped the leadership of Council to solve a perplexing political problem.[10]

The planners' bulwark against the strong political forces operating in the recreation area are facilities standards, or specifications regarding the number and size of facilities that are needed to serve a given size population (e.g., one playground for every 12,000 to 15,000 people). These standards, devised by professionals in the field, were the basis for the city facilities plan for recreation commissioned by the Planning Commission in 1957 and later incorporated into the 1960 Comprehensive Plan. More recently the staff of the Planning Commission devised a point rating system for comparing the level of existing and proposed recreation facilities in various neighborhoods. Each playground, tennis court, and swimming pool was assigned a point total depending on the number of participants it could serve at any one time. For example, a ballfield received 18 points (representing two teams of 9 players each), a tennis court 4 points, a swimming pool 100 points, etc. If the facility was lighted, the rating was increased by 50% to reflect the fact that it would get more use than an unlighted facility.

After totaling the points assigned to all existing recreation areas, the Planning Commission mapped their distribution. As of 1979, they concluded, there were few parts of the city with urgent unmet needs for new or expanded facilities.[11]

Applying these objective standards would appear to be quite a straightforward exercise. One simply compares the location, number, and size of existing facilities to the standards that are dictated by the population distribution; future construction is then aimed at filling in the gaps. And yet, the mere identification of areas where gaps exist does not constitute capital programming, because it does not dictate the order of priority for filling in these gaps. Thus, even though recreation planners consistently invoke professionally determined standards as their rationale for various projects, other considerations must also enter into the final calculation.

There is typically little or no conflict between the Planning Commission and the recreation department in the development of new capital projects. Since the city's recreation program is centered on building facilities and developing open spaces, its activities have always been perceived by the Planning Commission as an integral part of land-use planning. Throughout most of the postwar period, therefore, the commission has maintained especially close communication with the recreation department, and the two units have normally presented a united front before city council.

The council, for its part, has become increasingly vocal in challenging the priorities set by the Planning Commission. During the mid-1970s, as the budgetary pressures on the city government increased, a practice developed of deliberately including more recreation projects in the capital program than could possibly be built. Table 5.1 compares the amounts proposed by the Planning Commission and the amounts adopted by the city council in several recent capital programs. It shows the council's tendency to insert its own projects beyond what the commission recommends. Thus some projects, although approved by the council, simply go unfunded by the administration. This practice has the advantage of appeasing constituencies at the time of budget formulation, while still maintaining the city's fiscal solvency. Tacitly accepted by both the council and the city administration, this system involves carrying unbuilt projects in the budget for years at a time. Admittedly it frustrates neighborhood groups who have managed to secure places for their pet projects in the capital program and yet cannot get them built. But in the late 1970s and early

1980s this informal arrangement seemed to be one with which the council could live indefinitely.

The breach in the unspoken agreement finally came in the 1982–83 capital program, from the administration side rather than from the legislative side. In a dramatic departure from its past practices, the Planning Commission and mayor transmitted in spring 1982 an annual capital budget to council that contained not a single new recreation facility. The $20 million in recreation funding included in the proposed budget for 1982–83 was entirely earmarked for rehabilitation and upgrading of existing facilities. Presenting this austere budget to the city council, the mayor could not resist chiding the legislators for their profligacy in previous years. In 1981–82, for example, the council had added 147 new recreation projects totaling $18.5 million to the capital budget that the mayor and Planning Commission had proposed. The problem with such additions, according to the city's chief executive, was simply that there were no additional operating funds available to staff and maintain new facilities, and therefore no point in including any new construction in the budget ordinance. In fact, he warned, it might soon be necessary to begin closing some recreation facilities and branch libraries, just to keep an adequate level of services in those that remained open.

The administration's emphasis on rehabilitation over construction was supported not only by the Planning Commission but by a

**Table 5.1**

Budgets for Play Facilities in Three Recent Capital Programs

|  | As Proposed by Planning Commission | As Adopted by City Council |
| --- | --- | --- |
| 1982–87 Capital Program |  |  |
| Number of projects | 78 | 144 |
| Capital costs (millions) | $22 | $44 |
| 1983–88 Capital Program |  |  |
| Number of projects | 94 | 161 |
| Capital costs (millions) | $30 | $57 |
| 1984–89 Capital Program |  |  |
| Number of projects | 58 | 152 |
| Capital costs (millions) | $32 | $54 |

*Source:* Pennsylvania Economy League, *An Evaluation of the Capital Programming Process for the City of Philadelphia, with Emphasis on the Recreation/Culture Function,* Philadelphia, March 1984, p. 23.

large segment of the public. A 1982 survey of Philadelphia residents commissioned by the city's commissioner of recreation showed that when asked about the relative importance of improving maintenance on *existing* facilities, as compared with building *new* facilities, respondents gave much stronger support to the former than to the latter. Moreover, the preference for maintenance over new construction was just as strong among those respondents classified as frequent users of the city's recreation facilities as among those classified as nonusers. In other words, even those who would be most likely to benefit from the addition of new facilities believed that the city's funds would be better spent in maintaining existing ones.[12]

Employees of the recreation department who were surveyed in the same study also opposed construction of new facilities without additional staffing. During the 1970s, while the city had constructed 46 playgrounds and recreation centers, 52 new swimming pools, and 11 city gymnasiums, the number of recreation department employees had fallen by 30% and the ratio of employees per playground had declined by 47%. By the early 1980s, recreation employees obviously feared that their jobs would be made even more difficult if the staff for any new facilities were to be drawn away from existing facilities.[13] (The opinion expressed by recreation department staff in this survey coincides with the views of spokesmen for several public employee unions in Philadelphia. At least one of them, an AFSCME local, has even tried to negotiate with the city to include in the contract a provision prohibiting the city from opening new facilities without hiring additional staff to operate them.)

Even in the face of support for the rehabilitation approach among the general public as well as among public employees, the council remained unconvinced of the need to forego new construction. Council members were particularly outraged that the mayor and the Planning Commission proposed to discard projects that had already appeared in previous capital budgets but had not yet been built. Unwilling to accept this sudden departure from their established practice, the council responded by withdrawing some of the commission's proposals and inserting over 100 additional recreation projects totaling about $20 million; about half were previously approved and half were new projects. When the mayor received this revised budget to sign, he exercised his line-item veto to eliminate 52 of the newly inserted projects, but the council in turn responded by voting within hours to override the mayor's veto. The council's solidarity in defending its prerogatives was obvious from the vote total: 15 to 0.

In public exchanges about the proposed moratorium on new construction, the mayor accused council members of playing pork-barrel politics with the city's fragile budget, while the legislators in turn charged the mayor with wanting to turn the council into his "rubber stamp." And yet their disagreement was more than a matter of defending institutional prerogatives. The council clearly perceived its role in this conflict as Petshek had described it: protector of the average person in the neighborhood against the financial and business interests promoting downtown construction. In defending the council's refusal to accept a moratorium on recreation construction, the president of the council pointed to a "very basic difference in monetary and social philosophy":

> The administration's philosophy seems to be determined to continue to pour money into the Center City area at the expense of the neighborhoods. City Council, on the other hand, feels that neighborhoods have been neglected far too long (as evidenced by all of these unbuilt projects).[14]

Not content simply to see their projects included in the capital budget, as they had been in past years, the council then took an unprecedented step to try to insure that construction on those projects would actually begin during the year. Their leverage on the executive was the bond issue that was to be floated in order to pay for the 1982–83 capital program. When the mayor sent the loan-authorization bill to the council, the members threatened to withhold approval until they received a written assurance that their recreation projects would not be shunted aside as in previous years. Not until the city's managing director and finance director provided that assurance did the council approve the bond issue so that it could be put to a public referendum.

The struggle between the legislative and executive branches even extended to individual projects. When, for example, seven months into the budget year, the administration had not yet begun work on a project to extend a small park in the northwest section of the city and to install benches for the elderly, the council passed a bill authorizing a $400,000 expenditure for that specific purpose. Predictably, the mayor vetoed the bill, reiterating in his veto message that "the legislation involves the expenditure of public funds for new recreation land at a time when many current recreation facilities are understaffed, in severe disrepair, and in need of improvements."[15] Equally predictable was the council's overwhelming vote to override the veto: 15 to 1.

By the time of the hearings on the subsequent year's capital budget in spring 1983, it was obvious that the administration had decided not to proceed with 111 recreation department projects that had been included in the 1982–83 budget. Although they had been slated for construction and had even been included in the bond issue floated to finance the capital program, the projects had not been undertaken and, what is more, had been dropped from the proposed 1983–84 capital budget transmitted to the council by the mayor and the Planning Commission. As in the previous year, the administration recommended concentrating limited resources on renovating existing recreation centers. The infuriated response of council members echoed the theme of earlier debates. Condemning the imbalance between neighborhood projects and downtown projects, one council member representing North Philadelphia's poorest neighborhoods exploded: "I don't call that a program that reflects any interest in the residents of this city. We pay and we pay and we pay, and all we see is fancy buildings going up in the center of town."[16]

This time, however, the city's financial situation was such that the mayor could not afford to take the path he had taken the previous year (i.e., to exercise his line-item veto, only to be overridden by the irate council). The difference was that this time, the capital projects being proposed by the mayor and the Planning Commission would by themselves have pushed the city up to the debt limit imposed by the state. This time, it would be legally impossible for the council to insert additional recreation projects without eliminating an equivalent amount of borrowing from the administration's other projects. Once the council president made clear his intention to do just that, the administration quickly agreed to make its own cuts in order to free up funds for some council-sponsored recreation projects.

In 1984 a new mayor brought a new approach to his negotiations with the city council on the capital budget. Wilson Goode, known for his pragmatic style as a manager, adopted a distinctly conciliatory posture toward the council in seeking approval for his first capital budget, assuring the council that he would concentrate on moving the tremendous backlog of recreation projects in their districts; that he had created an administration team to periodically update the council on the progress of various projects of interests to its members; and that the council would receive a status report on the various projects every two months. At the same time Mayor Goode cautioned restraint in budgeting new recreation projects. The results of this attempt at diplomacy are clear from the figures we saw in table 5.1. It didn't work. The city council almost tripled the number of recreation projects proposed by the administration. As finally adopted, the recreation portion of the 1984–89 capital program added an estimated $7.5 million annually to the city's operating budget— $5.5 million in debt service plus an additional $2 million in operating expenses to staff the new and expanded recreation facilities.[17]

Preparing for the subsequent year's capital budget, the Planning Commission issued in January 1985 a strongly worded position paper alerting the mayor and city council that "the time has come to devote our attention to rebuilding what we already have. . . . Warnings about the city's crumbling infrastructure have gone unheeded, and the cost of compensating for deferred maintenance is growing." The commission report described retaining walls along the Schuylkill River's banks that were falling into the river, bridges so corroded that they could no longer safely carry their posted weights, and a health center in North Philadelphia that needed replacing because it was structurally unsound. To properly maintain all of the city's facilities, the commission estimated, would cost over $550 million a year, yet the city had been spending only about half that amount in the previous ten years.

Neither the commission report nor the mayor's pleas dissuaded the council from once again adding $10.6 million in new recreation projects to the proposed capital program. And when the commission announced its official opposition to these additional expenditures, the council retaliated by withdrawing $100,000 from the commission's operating budget for the year. The president of the council explained. "We don't intend to destroy the agency. We just intend to let them know that we don't like what goes on."[18]

Another year brought an even more strident warning from the Planning Commission, whose February 1986 report contemplated the need to begin closing down recreation centers in neighborhoods that had lost substantial population: "Rather than continuing to invest in these facilities for the benefit of the remaining few users, perhaps we should close them so that scarce capital and operating dollars can be more efficiently used." The commission's dire prediction was reinforced by dramatic coverage in the *Philadelphia Inquirer* of the cuts suffered by one particular recreation center located in a white working-class neighborhood in upper North Philadelphia. The city's standards for multipurpose recreation centers stipulated that the Olney Center should be staffed by at least three full-time and three part-time employees. But in fact, the center had in January 1986 only one full-time and one part-time staff member. When the one full-time employee was out of the building, it simply closed. Saturday activities had to be eliminated because of lack of staff, and no longer did the center open its gym for free play, because there was no adequate supervision to keep fights from breaking out. Termites were eating the gym floor, bleachers were falling apart, and the electrical scoreboard had not operated for three years. The newspaper story was accompanied by a photograph of parents, players, and coaches huddled in the January cold at the center's dimly lit entrance in the late afternoon, waiting for the only staff member to open it up for a scheduled basketball game. Although a 1983 consultant's study had detailed over $450,000 worth of capital repairs and improvements that needed to be made at the Olney Recreation Center, no such expenditures were scheduled until 1991 at the earliest.

When the mayor once more sent to the council his annual plea against funding new recreation facilities, the *Philadelphia Inquirer* strongly supported him. As in previous years, the plea fell on deaf ears. Again the mayor failed to dissuade the council from inserting an additional $10 million in projects throughout their districts. To make room for its preferred projects, the council cut funds for a new computer-aided dispatch system for city police, improvements to fire halls, police stations, and district health centers, improved street lighting and street signs, and improvements at the city's sports stadium and major park. With an editorial titled "Council's Capital Budget is Mostly Slush and Pork," the city's largest newspaper castigated the council for "running roughshod over attempts by Mayor Goode and the City Planning Commission to set responsible priorities in the capital budget."[19]

The increasingly strident tone in the annual confrontation over the recreation budget might lead an observer to believe that recreation is the most significant piece of the capital program. In fact, recreational and cultural projects account for only about 4% of the average capital program. Furthermore, the outcome of the struggle in the city council does not even determine how much the city spends. As I reported in chapter 2, there is a growing gap between the adopted budget and the city's spending pattern. In recent years the city administration has ended up spending less than half the funds authorized for recreation projects. Yet the annual battle has assumed enormous symbolic importance as a test of the city council's ability to control the formulation of the budget document. And while the council has consistently won the public political battle, it has not succeeded in controlling the construction program.


## SCHOOLS

Although school facilities constitute the single most important category of public facilities built in the city's neighborhoods, the school district's capital program has not been closely coordinated with the city's. Nor, for that matter, has any aspect of school policy been closely coordinated with city policy. The two major institutions of local government, in fact, have a long history of indifference to one another that continues right up to the present day, despite a long standing tradition of municipal control over the school district's budget and constant pressure from ward politicians for access to patronage jobs in the schools. Since the early part of the twentieth century, the city council has been responsible for levying property taxes to fund the schools within strict limits set by the state legislature. Throughout the 1940s and 1950s, however, the district's budgetary policy was dictated by its business manager, a conservative, unimaginative, and highly political individual who dominated a string of weak superintendents.[20] He remained in favor with party politicians as well as the city's business community by maintaining a low-cost operation and using school district patronage to best advantage. As a result of his policies the district's building program and its maintenance operation lagged badly behind the needed level, and the physical plant deteriorated. The schools remained virtually untouched by the reform wave that swept through Philadelphia's municipal government in the 1950s. The enthusiasm for physical planning, which was the hallmark of the reform administrations of Mayors Clark and Dilworth, simply did not affect school facilities planning.

It appears in retrospect that the blame for this separation lay on both sides. Clearly, the district's leadership was not eager to have its well-established routines disrupted by the planning "zealots" of the Clark and Dilworth administrations. Yet there is evidence that the bright young professionals installed in the City Planning Commission in the 1950s also preferred to avoid contact with the school district's murky patronage bureaucracy, even though they were constantly urged to make such contact by the Citizens' Council on City Planning (CCCP). The CCCP, it will be remembered, was the organization of citizen activists whose review and comments on the annual capital program were solicited every year throughout the 1950s and 1960s. There was more than a trace of exasperation in the following retort, made by the CCCP's executive director in 1962 concerning the Planning Commission's resistance to coordinating its activities with the school district's:

> It is inconceivable . . . that in a period of 20 years, the planners could have made so few inroads into the Board of Education's planning processes as has apparently been the case, if the planners were interested in trying to inject the planning process into school development and to treat schools as an essential element in the city planning process.[21]

Change finally came to Philadelphia's school district only after its all-powerful business manager died in 1962, although it is likely that even if he had lived, the district would have been forced to respond to the mounting discontent. Only a few months before his death, the prestigious Greater Philadelphia Movement (GPM) had issued the highly critical conclusions of its two-year study of the schools. The GPM, an organization composed of about one hundred of the city's top business executives, was the single most powerful civic organization in the community. Their newly awakened interest in the schools in the early 1960s signaled the start of a tumultuous decade for the stagnant educational machinery. The GPM study chided the city's establishment for being "apathetic about public education," noting that "the civic community has been encouraged to concentrate on city government reform, urban renewal, and city planning."[22] The deteriorated condition of school facilities was of special concern to the black community, as evidenced by a 1962 report submitted to the school board by the Philadelphia Urban League. It complained about severe school overcrowding in some neighborhoods where the black population had recently increased, while at the same time schools in some white neighborhoods were underutilized. Black activists used the occasion of the Urban League's report to the board to mount a public protest about the poor condition of school buildings in their communities.[23]

The widely diverse interests supporting school reform gathered enough momentum to force the state government in 1963 to establish an Educational Home Rule Charter Commission, whose reform proposals were ready for public referendum by spring 1965. The voters easily approved this new addition to the city's Home Rule Charter. The major structural changes it produced were: (1) to transfer the power to appoint school board members out of the Court of Common Pleas and into the hands of the mayor, and (2) to eliminate the state legislature's power to review and approve all increases in property taxes levied by the city council on behalf of the schools. From 1965 on, the city council could exercise total control over the rate of school taxation, without consulting the state.

Richardson Dilworth, the reform Democrat who had resigned the mayoralty to run unsuccessfully for governor, assumed the presidency of the reorganized school board and immediately set in motion a period of dramatic and controversial change. He called for a systematic survey of enrollment projections and school capacity to establish the magnitude of the district's "facilities gap." The district's capital program was now, for the first time, to be prepared in parallel with the city's capital program. The Educational Home Rule Charter Supplement of 1965 called for a one-year capital budget and a six-year capital program, both to be presented annually for board approval, just as the city's capital budget and six-year program were presented annually to the city council. Among the dozens of reform-minded young professionals Dilworth brought into the school bureaucracy was a planner from the Planning Commission, Graham Finney, who was made deputy superintendent for planning. His job was to guide the massive capital program that would be needed to rebuild the crumbling system. Already in May 1966, the district managed to pass a $60 million bond issue—the first step in what was projected to be a six-year, $420 million building program.

Interviewed a decade later about the early years of the Dilworth Board, Finney was reserved in his assessment of the program he had helped to shape:

> We were probably too successful in getting an enormous number of things underway in that heady period when money and attention and, for a moment, community support were all focused on the schools so that on the building front we sustained back-to-back $60 to $90 million dollar bond issues without too much difficulty.[24]

Among the reasons for Finney's reservations about the enormous building program of the late 1960s was undoubtedly the backlash that it prompted from white voters. For the facilities problems faced by the reformed board were not merely issues of capacity; they were, in Finney's own words, "entirely overlain by racial segregation issues."[25]

Hence, the Dilworth building program was heavily focused on poor black areas of the city. Like other policies of the new school administration, the construction program was widely perceived among Philadelphia voters as biased toward the black community. That perception, combined with increasing cost burdens placed on taxpayers, led to growing resistance to the new board's plans, especially from white working-class neighborhoods where many families sent their children to Catholic schools.

An unmistakable signal was sent to the progressive school administration from just such neighborhoods in spring 1969, when voters for the first time in decades rejected a $90 million school bond issue. Electoral returns showed that with the exception of a few traditionally liberal strongholds, no white wards supported the issue, while all black wards approved it.[26] The school board's own analyst explained the unexpected failure this way: "There was a feeling that the black community was getting all the improvements at the expense of the whites."[27]

White backlash, however, is not the only reason to view the massive school building program of the late 1960s and early 1970s with reservations. Another reason is that the heavy focus on inner city neighborhoods meant that school district investments were made in precisely those areas that sustained heavy population losses during the 1970s. Of the 108 capital projects completed by the school district from 1967 through 1971 (the peak years of the Dilworth construction program), over half were investments in neighborhoods that suffered higher-than-average losses in school-age population during the 1970s.

In fact, throughout the postwar period, the school district invested disproportionately in neighborhoods that subsequently lost much of their school-age population. Table 5.2 shows the zero-order correlations between school capital investments in each of the three

**Table 5.2**

Correlations between Investments in Schools and Change in School-Age Population

| | Change in School-Age Population | | |
|---|---|---|---|
| *Facilities Spending* | *1950s* | *1960s* | *1970s* |
|---|---|---|---|
| 1950s | +.239* | −.171** | — |
| 1960s | — | +.340* | −.326* |
| 1970s | — | — | −.278* |

*Significant at the .01 level.
**Significant at the .05 level.

postwar decades, and change in the size of the neighborhood's school-age population. It shows for the 1950s and 1960s a positive correlation between spending and change in the school-age population during the decade when spending actually took place. In other words, there was some tendency for capital spending to be channeled to neighborhoods whose population was at that point increasing, or at least declining less than the average Philadelphia neighborhood. But note that in both cases, the correlation changes to a negative sign in the subsequent decade, indicating that the pattern of investment tended to favor neighborhoods that then lost school population in the succeeding decade.

How is it possible that the neighborhoods receiving high levels of spending could be gaining school-age population during one decade and losing it during the next? The data suggest that in a significant number of neighborhoods, the influx of large numbers of black households brought sizable increases in the school-age population. And in many cases, a dramatic changeover of neighborhoods from white to black during one decade was followed by substantial population losses during the subsequent decade. It is in precisely these kinds of neighborhoods, where the black population was rapidly increasing, that political pressure for increased school investment was focused during the 1960s. Thus, it is not surprising that the strongest relationship in the table is the negative one between school spending in the 1960s and population changes in the 1970s. Since the greatest proportion of 1960s capital spending was undertaken in the latter half of the decade by the Dilworth board, we would expect the data to reflect that board's priority on inner city neighborhoods (which tended to be big population losers in the 1970s). Note also that by the 1970s the board was investing in areas that were already losing school-age population, even as the investments were being made.

Given such a trend, it is hardly surprising that by the early 1980s, the excess capacity of some schools, and of the system in general, had become too obvious to ignore. By the 1981–82 school year, the district had about 16% more classroom space in its schools than it needed, and projections indicated that the excess capacity would almost double by the 1987–88 school year, if nothing were done. (See table 5.3) Faced with this prospect, the board made an initial attempt to close about ten schools in May 1982, but quickly withdrew the plan in the face of an overwhelming public protest.

Shifting its strategy, the board formed an assessment committee to undertake a comprehensive study of excess capacity, and to recommend closings on the basis of uniform criteria, including under-utilized classroom space, the age and condition of buildings and the needed repairs, and the lack of facilities such as gymnasiums and cafeterias. The board's hope was obviously to prepare a more solid financial case for the closings, in order to meet the inevitable pressure from parents and community groups. The assessment committee was structured to include all the major interests; it included members of the school board and city council, staff planners from the school district and the City Planning Commission, parents, and community representatives. But in the end, despite the committee's work, the decision was strongly influenced by political considerations. The committee's report recommended closing fourteen schools, and as soon as the list was made public, pressure began mounting on behalf of the targeted schools. As in other cities where school closings have been tried, the suggestion was seen by parents and other local residents as a blow to the integrity of the neighborhood as a social unit.[28] Protests against the closings were not confined to the hundreds of parents who packed school board meetings, but extended to the arena of electoral politics as well. Chief among the protesters was a handful of city council members who, despite the council's representation on the assessment committee recommending the closings, still objected to them. The basis of their opposition was primarily the damage that neighborhoods would suffer, once the neighborhood school had closed. Several state legislators representing Philadelphia districts also opposed the closings, despite the fact that the legislature had been warning the Philadelphia School District for years about the need to tighten its belt financially.

On the school issue, as on the city's capital program, the mayor argued forcefully for the need to cut costs, even if it meant closing down neighborhood facilities. Thus, the school closing controversy developed along much the same lines as the debate over recreation

**Table 5.3**

Excess Capacity of Philadelphia Schools

|  | 1981–82 | 1987–88 |
|---|---|---|
| Capacity of schools | 247,326 | 247,326 |
| Students enrolled | 207,412 | 174,220 |
| Excess capacity | 39,914 | 73,106 |
| Percent of capacity unused | 16% | 30% |

*Source:* Philadelphia City Planning Commission, *Profile of Public Schools,* Philadelphia, September 1982.

facilities, with the administrators in charge of facilities (principally, the superintendent of schools and the mayor) favoring cutbacks, while the electoral representatives of the neighborhoods in both the city council and the state legislature, opposed them. In the end, the board bowed to political pressure and voted to close only half of the fourteen schools originally recommended by the committee, leading the *Philadelphia Inquirer* to editorialize that the board had "flunked an important test of fiscal responsibility."[29]

Several of the city's vacant schools have been converted to other uses. The former Hawthorne Elementary School in South Philadelphia, for example, has been transformed into fifty-five apartments for the elderly and disabled. A neighborhood organization in the working-class area sought and received low-interest loans from four different sources to support the conversion: the United States Department of Housing and Urban Development ($350,000); Cigna Corporation, a Philadelphia-based insurance and financial services firm ($435,000); Philadelphia Housing Development Corporation, a local nonprofit agency ($550,000); and the Enterprise Foundation of Baltimore, another nonprofit that assists neighborhood organizations ($540,000). The one-bedroom apartments were earmarked for neighborhood residents, especially the elderly. Not all such conversions have been enthusiastically greeted by nearby residents. In spite of the blighting effects of vacant school buildings, residents' groups have frequently opposed the school board's efforts to transfer them to other uses. Neighbors have especially resisted plans to convert the old schools to shelters for the homeless or homes for the retarded. Yet even some proposals for more traditional housing projects have met community opposition, particularly housing that is likely to bring more school-age youngsters into an area.


## IS SERVICE CONSOLIDATION POSSIBLE?


Knowing what dramatic population losses have been suffered by some inner city neighborhoods in the postwar period, and especially in the 1970s, we might wonder why school and city officials should face such difficulty in cutting back on public facilities. After all, the public image projected in the media is one of "bombed out" sections of the inner city where whole blocks have been abandoned. If, as has been suggested, there are sections of the city that have been virtually evacuated, why should public officials find it difficult to shut down the facilities that serve them? Indeed, there are even planners in Philadelphia and other aging industrial cities who have argued that massive population losses from some inner city neighborhoods create opportunities for more efficient public services. By publicly acquiring large tracts of land, once they have been abandoned, the city government could redevelop them into open spaces or industrial parks, while at the same time confining public services to those sections that remain populated.[30]

The problem with this optimistic scenario is that it is based on media images of the inner city, not on the reality. Census reports have focused our attention on how many people have left the inner city, ignoring the equally important question of how many people remain behind. Table 5.4 lists the 21 neighborhoods that suffered population losses of 30 or more persons per acre in the period 1950 to 1980. The table also displays the density of the population remaining in each of

**Table 5.4**

Philadelphia Neighborhoods Showing Largest Population Losses, 1950 to 1980

|  | *Population Loss,*<br>*1950 to 1980*<br>*(persons/acre)* | *Population*<br>*Density 1980*<br>*(persons/acre)* |
|---|---|---|
| Temple University | 79 | 31 |
| Cabot | 56 | 40 |
| Wharton | 53 | 54 |
| Poplar | 52 | 22 |
| Fairmount/Francisville | 51 | 49 |
| Point Breeze | 50 | 59 |
| North Central | 47 | 57 |
| Queen Village | 47 | 39 |
| Powelton/Mantua | 43 | 38 |
| S.W. Center City | 42 | 47 |
| Pennsport | 40 | 51 |
| Strawberry Mansion II | 38 | 58 |
| Hartranft | 37 | 41 |
| S. Broad Street | 36 | 61 |
| Brewerytown | 36 | 52 |
| Grays Ferry | 34 | 44 |
| Whitman | 32 | 68 |
| Northern Liberties | 32 | 20 |
| Olde City | 31 | 5 |
| Belmont | 30 | 34 |
| Passyunk | 30 | 65 |
| Citywide average | 12 | 31 |

these communities in 1980. The juxtaposition of the two columns demonstrates a critical point often overlooked in the debates about urban depopulation—namely, that the greatest losses have occurred in the most heavily-populated sections of the city. Hence, these sections have retained extremely high densities even after massive outmigration. By 1980, only three of the areas listed in table 5.4 had dropped below the average citywide density for residential areas (i.e., 31 persons per acre), and most of them still showed densities one-and-a-half to two times greater than the citywide average. In short, the data do not support the feasibility of basing a cutback strategy on the expectation that some neighborhoods are simply going to empty out.

Nor is the idea of consolidating services in the more heavily populated neighborhoods an ideal strategy. Researchers looking at the location of public facilities have sometimes concluded that too high a concentration of service sites can cause problems. One study of Philadelphia identified district geographic clusters of social services. Wherever a public health center was located, the researchers were likely to find also, in close proximity, these other service sites: welfare/employment center, day care center, community center, psychiatric center, legal counseling, and human relations/social action center. This clustering of sites together, they speculated, may not be an unmixed blessing to the residents. In fact, the community may suffer from the presence of

> facilities which remind residents of their dependent status and transform the aspect of the community from that of a residential place to a hub for the provision of service for the dependent, the disabled, and the downwardly mobile. This subtle change in the perceived function of the community may weaken residential values and hasten a decline in the actual function.[31]

Other researchers have made the same point. One of them, writing from a political economy perspective, has even suggested that the concentration of service facilities in poor neighborhoods—a trend that ultimately has negative consequences for the area—is not an unintended outcome, but rather a deliberate, functional, and convenient way of confining service-dependent populations to enclaves in the inner city.[32] The residents of city districts where public services are clustered are increasingly vocal in opposing further institutional encroachment on residential land. Obviously, certain kinds of land uses (for example, community shelters for abused spouses, homeless and deinstitutionalized persons) are particularly likely to draw a negative reaction from neighbors.[33] Yet even some traditionally acceptable facilities, like public schools, pools, and playgrounds can be viewed as magnets for troublesome teenagers and therefore undesirable additions to the neighborhood, especially if the area already contains other public facilities. Some neighborhood associations have taken the position before the zoning board that they wish to exclude *any* new institutional uses in their communities, no matter how innocuous. The problem, as they see it, is as much the density of institutions as their character.

## CONCLUSION

In this chapter I have dwelt on two case studies of recreation and school facilities planning because they illustrate so clearly that the answer to the question, Is Philadelphia overcapitalized? depends entirely on where you sit. Traditional budget analyses have portrayed bureaucratic administrators as constantly seeking to enlarge their domains by adding new facilities. This is the starting assumption, for example, in Pagano and Moore's study of capital budgeting in nine cities. They describe the city council as the major force restraining capital expenditures because council members want to avoid raising taxes.[34] Yet their assumptions, drawn from the literature on budgeting processes, do not fit Philadelphia under conditions of scarcity; here, the roles they describe for bureaucrats and council members appear to be reversed.

From the viewpoint of facilities administrators who are forced to staff and equip all the existing service sites on ever-tighter operating budgets, the obvious solution is to close down some sites, in order to concentrate resources on the remaining sites. At a minimum, administrators argue, the city must refrain from building more sites that will force them to spread operating money even further. And yet the fact that one of the city's major governmental institutions—the city council—is geographically based makes it almost impossible to select the neighborhoods for cuts. Such selective cuts would be difficult to accomplish under any circumstances. What makes them even harder to "sell" to council members and their constituents in the present environment is the widespread perception that city administrators are continuing to pour tax dollars into a number of gigantic commercial renewal projects at the very time when neighborhood facilities are being shut down. Council members have increasingly viewed the capital program as a zero-sum game in which major citywide projects are being built at the expense of their constituents in the neighborhoods. How appropriate is the zero-sum game as a metaphor for capital planning? That is the subject of the next chapter, in which I shall consider the financing of Philadelphia's capital budget.

# Financing Capital Projects

T HE various disinvestment models outlined in chapter 1 share a common weakness that limits their usefulness for predicting the balance of resources going to poor versus affluent neighborhoods. As they are usually formulated, these models focus too narrowly on the competition *among neighborhoods* for public expenditures. They assume that city officials have developed (either formally or informally) some "hierarchy of neighborhoods," on the basis of which they plot investments. The city's poorest sections, according to the model, invariably lose in the competition for limited funds.[1] But our figures show that in the competition among neighborhoods, the lowest-income neighborhoods, while they did not fare particularly well in the 1950s, fared extremely well in the 1960s and 1970s.

By restricting our view to the competition among neighborhoods, however, we are losing sight of an important question: What proportion of the entire capital budget was devoted to neighborhood facilities as a whole? Only a portion of the city's capital expenditures goes for neighborhood projects. The city also invests in many projects that are located in the central business district. In fact a great deal of the literature on urban decay and renewal has emphasized the bias toward downtown development as the predominant response by city governments—a response that has robbed the neighborhoods of their fair share of redevelopment dollars and, what is worse, has displaced the poor in order to create gentrified enclaves near the business district. Seen in this light, the major political fault line in urban renewal is that which pits neighborhoods against downtown.[2]

The competition between downtown and the neighborhoods is a central theme of Philadelphia politicians and neighborhood leaders. Since the city's neighborhood movement gathered momentum in the early 1970s, its leaders have continually criticized the city for the imbalance between investments in downtown development and in neighborhood development. Community activists have charged that gentrifying sections of center city have drawn many of their new residents from already weakened neighborhoods, and that center city commercial development has eroded the smaller shopping districts that are more convenient to neighborhood residents.

Society Hill, the elegantly restored quarter of eighteenth-century homes in the historic heart of the city, symbolizes to many Philadelphians the disproportionate emphasis placed by the city on downtown development. Particularly galling to many groups within the city is the fact that most of the benefits of center city renewal were reserved for the upper-middle-class families who could afford to buy or rent the extravagantly priced restorations. A number of commentators on the Society Hill renewal project have pointed out that its upper-class bias was by no means an unintended outcome, but instead the prevailing conception of the project from the start.[3] The upwardly mobile professionals for whom the historic houses were rehabilitated were identified as the core market for the shops, cultural institutions, restaurants, and entertainment spots that were to be developed in the reviving city center. Their presence in large numbers in the downtown area, it was hoped, would fuel the nascent trend toward white-collar employment in the CBD. Thus, the residential renaissance in Society Hill was coupled with another massive renewal effort, the Market Street East complex, which included a multilevel downtown shopping center known as the Gallery, a commuter rail tunnel to link the two major suburban rail networks serving the central business district, and several large office complexes. It is hardly surprising that this gigantic and widely publicized redevelopment effort in center city, which began in the mid-1950s and has continued to the present day, has been viewed by neighborhood activists as their major rival for public investment capital.

But the high visibility of center city projects has led many local observers to overlook another category of capital spending with even greater importance—that is, projects whose functions are citywide in scope, but that are not located downtown. Within this category fall investments in economic infrastructure—e.g., utilities,expressways, airport and port installations—as well as in the city's largest social service facilities—e.g., correctional centers, homes for the aged and for children, and, until the late 1970s, a municipal hospital. Because they are scattered throughout the city, projects in this category are not nearly so visible as the redevelopment efforts concentrated in the downtown area. Yet they constitute a major share of the city's capital budget.

## THE GROWING IMPORTANCE OF CITYWIDE PROJECTS

In order to weigh the relative importance of this third category of expenditures in recent capital budgets, I have analyzed the city's capital programs during three different six-year periods. The reader may recall that six years is the length of time covered by the capital program that the mayor submits each year to the city council, along with the one-year capital budget. The three periods—1954–1959, 1966–1971, and 1974–1979—were selected to represent three different mayoral administrations. In each case, the starting point is three years into the mayoral term, to allow sufficient time for the new leadership to have its own priorities reflected in the capital program. After all, construction projects often take several years from start to finish, and each new mayor has inevitably found himself completing projects that had been initiated by his predecessors. Figure 6.1 shows the relative shares of expenditures for projects completed in the neighborhoods, in center city, and also in our third category of citywide projects not located in center city. (Note that the data represent construction actually *completed*, rather than construction *planned* for these periods.)

The first period, 1954 to 1959, really spans two mayoral administrations, those of Joseph Clark and Richardson Dilworth. Yet the close political association between these two Democratic reform politicians, and their common goals of restoring good government and rebuilding downtown, justify their both being treated as advocates of a single reform platform. The late 1950s was a period of enormous investment in several downtown traffic arteries, improvements to subway stations in the central business district, and public improvements to complement the massive private-sector investment in the Penn Center office complex.[4] Yet despite the common perception that the reform administrations of the 1950s were heavily committed to downtown revival,

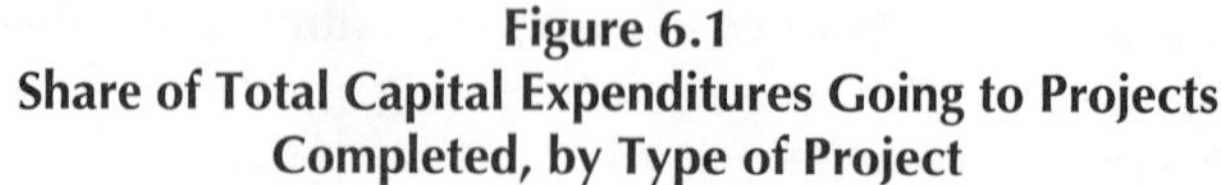

**Figure 6.1**
**Share of Total Capital Expenditures Going to Projects**
**Completed, by Type of Project**

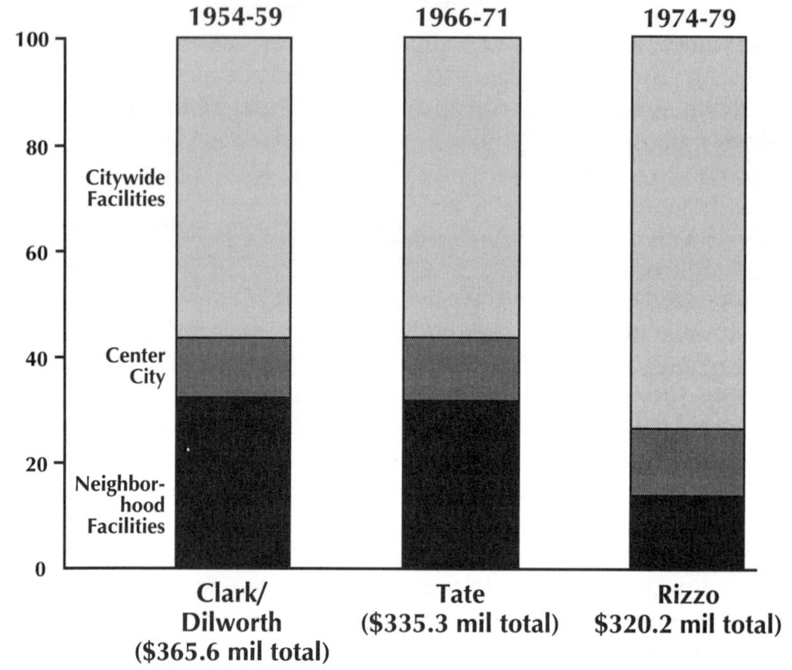

Note:
All dollar figures are adjusted for inflation, using the Bureau of Labor Statistics consumer price index, based on the 1967 value of the dollar. For a breakdown of the items contained in all three budget categories, see Appendix 1.

we can see that the proportion of the total program devoted to center city was actually slightly lower than in succeeding administrations.

Our second period, 1966 to 1971, came during the administration of James H. J. Tate, the city council president who became mayor after Mayor Richardson Dilworth resigned the mayoralty to run for governor. Tate then ran for the office on his own and was elected in 1963. Tate's background was in the regular Democratic organization, and his administration marked the end of the reform era in Philadelphia. Tate relied heavily on the labor unions, municipal workers, and traditional ward organizations, and was reputed to maintain their support by distributing the spoils of his office: city contracts, salary increases, favors, and services to faithful ward organizers.

The widespread and generous allocations for community facilities, which we noted earlier as a characteristic of the 1960s, were consistent with Tate's machine style of politics. Yet despite the striking differences between Tate's political style and that of the reformers who preceded him, we observe that the capital program pursued during his term was almost identical in its distribution among the three main categories of expenditures. The largest single project included in the "citywide" category during these years was Veterans' Stadium, a 66,000-seat sports stadium that required two separate bond issues: one for $25 million approved by voters in 1964 and another for $13 million approved in 1967. Other big-ticket items in this same category were the city's two airports, the gas works, the convention center, and the city's one major hospital.

The 1970s brought the administration of Frank Rizzo, Tate's hand-picked successor. Running on a law-and-order platform, Rizzo received strong support from the white working-class and middle-class neighborhoods of the city, though not from the black wards. His populist campaign stressed his concern for the preservation of neighborhoods and the neighborhood way of life. Indeed, a constant theme throughout his eight years in office was that neighborhoods should have the right to veto any new development that would substantially change their character. The most celebrated example was Mayor Rizzo's consistent defense of the right of one white working-class community in South Philadelphia, known as Whitman Park, to refuse to accept a publicly financed housing project for which both black and white families would be eligible. But figure 6.1 does not show a particularly strong commitment to neighborhood improvement. On the contrary, it documents an enormous increase in the share of capital expenditures going to citywide projects—an increase that came entirely at the expense of the neighborhood share, while leaving intact the share allocated to center city projects. During this six-year period, by far the largest item in the citywide category was the upgrading of pollution abatement equipment at the city's three water pollution control plants, designed to insure that treated water returned to the region's rivers would be clean enough to preserve health and safety standards. This one program alone, with a few other improvements to the water treatment plants, accounted for over 40% of the total allocation to citywide projects between 1974 and 1979. (See table in Appendix 1 for detailed breakdown.)

One other aspect of figure 6.1 deserves mention: the total dollar value of the Rizzo capital program in the 1970s is less than the Tate program of the 1960s, which is in turn smaller than the Clark/Dilworth program of the 1950s. Note that these dollar values have been adjusted to reflect the effects of inflation; while the nominal price tags on recent capital programs have been much larger than those of the 1950s, the erosion in purchasing power has more than equaled the increase in dollar amounts. What this means is that neighborhoods have lost ground over the decades, not only because their share of the total budget has declined, but also because the total budget itself has shrunk. In short, neighborhoods are not getting a smaller slice of a shrinking pie.

This finding leads us to question the emphasis that disinvestment theorists have placed on the competition among neighborhoods for public resources. With respect to the five types of community facilities examined in chapter 3, the low-income and minority sections of the city appeared in the 1970s to be attracting twice as large a share of the total dollars spent as they had received in the 1950s. But despite that increase, these disadvantaged neighborhoods actually lost ground because of the simultaneous cut in the total dollars being spent for neighborhood facilities. I conclude that low-income sections have received fewer dollars in recent capital budgets, not because the money has been channeled into facilities in the better-off neighborhoods. Rather, their allocations have gone down because the share devoted to uses other than neighborhood facilities has increased. Furthermore, within the category of non-neighborhood uses, the biggest increases have not come in center city development, but rather in the kinds of facilities whose function is citywide but whose location is outside of the central business district.

How do we account for the increased importance of the citywide category in Mayor Rizzo's investment program? The answer given by many neighborhood activists in the 1970s was a simple one— the political clout exercised by prodevelopment groups. Aware that the city was spending vast sums on public works while neglecting their communities, they concluded that the reason for the imbalance was their relative powerlessness. My own view is that there were other, more convincing explanations for the pattern of expenditures. By looking at the actual expenditures made in large-scale, citywide projects, we may gain some insight into the reasons for their prominence. As I have already mentioned, the largest single item was the pollution abatement program carried on at the city's three waste water treatment plants. Like many cities across the United States, Philadelphia began in the 1970s to upgrade its sewage treatment facilities in response to new regulations issued by the National Environmental Protection Agency, as well as by the Pennsylvania Department of Resources and the Delaware River Basin Commission. When work began in the mid-1970s on this upgrading, it was almost immediately obvious that the city would not meet the deadline of July 1, 1977 that had been imposed by the 1972 amendments to the Federal Water Control Act. The EPA reacted by filing suit in federal court against the city of Philadelphia, and after complex and extended litigation, the city finally signed a consent decree in May 1979 in which the court established a multiyear schedule for the completion of capital improvements to bring the city into compliance with all applicable limitations on effluents. By July 1979, the first of the city's three waste water treatment plants had been upgraded, and the other two were scheduled for completion in late 1983 and 1986.[5] In effect, the city had no choice but to spend a considerable share of its capital budget in this way.

Under the heading of expenditures by the municipally owned gas works, the largest single investment in the 1974–1979 program was a new synthetic natural gas plant capable of manufacturing gas from naphtha as a supplement to the gas supplies that were piped into Philadelphia from other parts of the country. For this project as well, the justification for replacing several very old oil-to-gas plants included the need to meet pollution control standards (although greater cost effectiveness was also an important rationale). Yet another example of environmental considerations was the city's program during the 1970s to reorganize its solid waste management efforts. An order from the Philadelphia Air Pollution Control Board required that the city take its polluting incinerators out of operation. To meet this order, the city closed all but two of its six incinerators. These two were then fitted with more effective pollution control equipment, while the four closed-down incinerator sites had to be converted to operate instead as storage and loading points for truck hauling to landfills. And despite these changes undertaken in the 1970s, the early 1980s brought a legal action against the city by the Pennsylvania Department of Environmental Resources, which claimed that one of the two reequipped incinerators continued to violate both air and water pollution standards.

These examples suggest that a major factor accounting for the prominence of citywide projects in the capital program of the 1970s was the demand for environmental protection. The other major types of expenditures included in the citywide category showed no dramatic departures in the 1970s from previous patterns. The city continued to invest in economic infrastructure (e.g., airports, port, civic center, roads, and bridges), and in its major service facilities (with the important exception of Philadelphia General Hospital, the city's only municipal hospital, which was shut down in the mid-1970s).

## SOURCES OF MUNICIPAL CAPITAL

Another important contributor to the dominance of large-scale, citywide projects has been the financing mechanisms available to support them. To appreciate the role played by financing mechanisms in influencing the pattern of municipal investments, we need first to understand the various sources from which capital funds flow. These are basically of three kinds. The first is current revenues and assets accumulated in cash reserves or revolving funds. Early in the city's history these were virtually the only ways for the municipality to pay for public improvements. But starting in the early nineteenth century, Philadelphia began to finance capital projects by a second means—borrowing—a practice that has continued to the present day. It is still theoretically possible for the city to finance public works from operating revenues, but in reality only a tiny percentage of the annual capital budget is supported by current revenues. Most construction is financed instead by issuing long-term bonds.

The justification for borrowing money to build public works is widely accepted among governments at all levels. By definition, capital projects have a long life and therefore are presumed to yield long-term benefits to the community. Yet the outlay of money to pay for these projects takes the form of a lump sum payment at the time of construction. Borrowing allows the city to spread the burden of the investment over an extended period of time, so that in future years the taxpayers who are enjoying the benefits will be paying a part of the cost. Most governments regard this as the fairest way to allocate the cost of facilities.

From a level of $50 million at the turn of the century, Philadelphia's total bonded indebtedness steadily increased until 1932, when the figure stood at $446 million. Then through the rest of the 1930s and into the 1940s, the city's borrowing power dropped, as real estate assessments declined. Not until 1952 did the debt climb back up to surpass its 1932 level. Since then the ambitious postwar rebuilding program, coupled with inflation, has tripled the debt, bringing it to $1.5 billion in 1985. Adding the school district's indebtedness brought the 1985 total to about $2 billion.[6]

The figures on total bonded indebtedness cover two distinct categories of borrowing, and the differences between the two have played a critical role in determining the course of Philadelphia's capital program. The first category is the debt that results from the issuing of "general obligation bonds," which the city pledges to repay out of general revenues (mostly from taxes, but also to a small extent from fees, fines, and a few other sources). In the language of the bond market, these issues are backed by the "full faith and credit" of the city government, meaning that city officials are legally obligated to use all methods at their disposal to insure that the debt is repaid on time. They would even be forced to cut programs or raise taxes, should these steps prove necessary in order to meet the loan schedule. The second kind of borrowing involves the issuing of "revenue bonds," or bonds to be repaid from revenues generated by the particular project being financed, rather than by tax revenues from the city's general fund.

The projects for which revenue bonds are floated are thus considered to be self-sustaining; that is, they are expected to create enough revenues for the city, in the form of service charges, rentals, and other fees, to retire the debt. Examples of this kind of project would be airport construction, port improvements, water and sewer lines for which user fees are charged, parking garages, and sports stadiums. Bond issues for such projects are based on the principle that only their users should be required to pay for them; the bonds are thus secured only by the earnings of the particular projects specified in the bond issue. They are not guaranteed, in the sense that they have no claim on the general taxing power of the city government. If the city were to default on a revenue bond, then the bondholders could take liens only against the facilities identified in the bond issue; they would not have a claim on any other city assets. For that reason, the city usually has to offer a slightly higher interest rate on these than on general obligation bonds.[7]

A major advantage of revenue bonds over general obligation bonds is that the former are not subject to any state limits, whereas the latter are closely regulated by a provision of the state constitution. According to that provision, Philadelphia is permitted to issue general obligation bonds only up to an amount that is equal to 13½% of the average of the previous ten years' assessments of taxable real estate. The effect of using the ten-year average is to make the city's borrowing power from year to year less directly dependent on assessments in that particular year. Hence, if assessments were to drop sharply or rise sharply as the result of reassessments in any given year, the debt ceiling would not immediately reflect the change in property values. (Obviously, this system reduces the city's temptation to reassess property values upward in order to secure greater borrowing power.) The state constitution also regulates the amount of general obligation debt that can be issued without the approval of Philadelphia voters. Within the 13½% limit, up to 3% may be incurred by the council's action alone; the other 10½% must be voter-approved debt.

In addition to current income and borrowing, the third source of capital funds is intergovernmental aid, chiefly from the federal government. The bulk of this aid is for investments in a limited number of areas, the major ones being (1) roads and highways, for which the federal share may be as high as 90%, (2) waste water systems, for which the federal share may reach 75%, (3) mass transit projects, with the federal share set at 90%, and(4) airport development, for which the federal share is 90%. Federal subsidies are thus extremely generous, but only for a limited number of investment categories, and generally for new construction instead of for repairs and rehabilitation. And frequently the subsidies are tied to specific federal directives. This is the case, for example, with the massive building program for water treatment facilities that Philadelphia undertook in the 1970s in response to new federally imposed environmental standards. The one recent case of a federal capital subsidy that permitted cities to exercise discretion in spending was the Local Public Works (LPW) program of the mid-1970s, intended by congress to provide economic stimulation to declining cities. This program distributed a total of $6 billion in capital funds during 1976 and 1977, according to an entitlement formula rather than on a project-by-project basis. Analysis showed that given a free hand in allocating the LPW funds, cities used almost half of the money to finance rehabilitation, repair, and expansion of existing facilities, instead of building new ones.[8] Despite this temporary program and some moves to incorporate repair and maintenance subsidies into federal transportation subsidies, the vast bulk of federal capital assistance is still geared to supporting new construction, not rehabilitation.

A perfect illustration of the impact of federal funds on Philadelphia's capital priorities is the building of the Chestnut Street Transitway, a project of the Rizzo administration that converted one of the busiest shopping streets in the downtown area into a pedestrian mall. Looking back on the origins of that project, Mayor Rizzo's director of commerce explained how it was selected:

> The Chestnut Street Transitway . . . had been on the books for a long time. It came to be built in the following way. Because of the relationship between Rizzo and Nixon, money was promised, six million outright to build the transitway in time for the Bicentennial (1976). The Nixon administration was primarily interested in building an in-city shopping mall to see how it worked. Because of the Nixon-Rizzo relationship, we got first crack at being the model. We asked the Chestnut Street merchants if they wanted the transitway. They said yes. So we took the money. So many of our decisions were based on where the money was; what the federal government would fund, we built.[9]

It would be hard to overstate the influence on urban capital programs of both the amounts and types of federal aid available. George Peterson has gone so far as to assert that "probably the most important generator of state-local capital investment trends has been the combination of federal aid and federal regulatory standards."[10]

## THE CITY'S PREFERENCE FOR SELF-SUSTAINING PROJECTS

Having outlined the major sources of funds for capital projects, let us now turn to an examination of the influence of the funding mechanisms on Philadelphia's capital program. When we compare the impact of the various funding options on the city's operating budget (and by extension on the prevailing tax rate), it is obvious that financing capital projects through general obligation bonds is the least attractive option for city officials. Projects that can generate enough revenue to be self-sustaining, or can attract federal and state subsidies to cover a majority of their costs, are simply easier to undertake, both in financial and political terms.

The preference for self-sustaining or federally subsidized projects is not a new feature of capital planning in Philadelphia. A study of Philadelphia's capital program during the 1950s identified this same tendency.[11] However, the stagnation of the city's tax base in the 1970s made it increasingly difficult for the city to take on new tax-supported debt. Table 6.1 shows the proportion of the capital programs in recent years that fell into the three main categories of tax-supported, self-sustaining, and subsidized by federal and state contributions. Although the balance among the three categories has fluctuated from program to program, the general trend is unmistakable: self-sustaining expenditures account for a rising share of the most recent programs, while both tax support and support from higher-level governments have declined as proportions of the total financing package.

Some important consequences flow from the trends documented in table 6.1. First, as the city's taxing capacity has stagnated in the past decade, the availability of funds from outside sources, principally from the federal government, has become increasingly critical in shaping the capital program. Because of the federal emphasis on new construction rather than on rehabilitation, the incentive to the city is to continue to build anew, even while the existing infrastructure deteriorates. So to the extent that the city has "overbuilt" in some services, (and that issue, as we saw in the last chapter, is a matter of contention in Philadelphia), then it is reasonable to see federal subsidies as a contributing factor.

Second, the types of construction favored by officials are those that can attract other types of funding besides local tax revenues. As an illustration, I have provided in table 6.2 a breakdown of the 1982–87 capital program adopted by the city government; it is typical of recent capital programs. The "Total" column on the right shows that by far

**Table 6.1**

Sources of Funds for Philadelphia Capital Programs

| Program Years | Tax-<br>supported | Self-<br>sustaining | Federal/<br>State |
|---|---|---|---|
| 1974–1979 | 15.8% | 20.9% | 59.5% |
| 1975–1980 | 16.0 | 16.9 | 65.3 |
| 1976–1981 | 17.1 | 21.4 | 59.0 |
| 1977–1982 | 15.9 | 22.1 | 59.2 |
| 1978–1983 | 17.1 | 27.6 | 53.3 |
| 1979–1984 | 13.2 | 26.7 | 58.1 |
| 1980–1985 | 12.3 | 26.2 | 58.8 |
| 1981–1986 | 12.0 | 34.7 | 50.2 |
| 1982–1987 | 12.7 | 33.4 | 51.9 |

*Source:* Philadelphia City Planning Commission, *Capital Program* (annual issues for the given years).

the largest items in this six-year capital program are transportation, services to property, and economic development. Note that in each of these three categories, the tax-supported contribution is minimal (9%, 2% and 11%, respectively). In the case of transportation, over 90% of the funds are expected to come from federal and state sources; both the categories of economic development and services to property (including fire, gas, water, and sewer services) are mostly self-sustaining, with a significant contribution from higher levels of government.

At this point it may have occurred to the reader that there might be a different explanation for the finding that the largest items in the

**Table 6.2**

Breakdown of 1982–1987 Capital Program, by Source of Funds, (in millions).

| | Tax-Supported | Self Sustaining | Revolving Funds | Federal, State, and Other Non-City Sources | Total |
|---|---|---|---|---|---|
| Culture and recreation | $84.1 (95%) | — | — | $4.4 (5%) | $88.5 (100%) |
| Economic development | 22.9 (11%) | 125.1 (58%) | 18.0 (8%) | 49.7 (23%) | 215.7 (100%) |
| Health | 10.3 (100%) | | | | 10.3 (100%) |
| Housing[2] | 38.2 (65%) | 6.6 (11%) | 13.7 (23%) | | 58.5 (100%) |
| Judiciary and law enforcement | 15.0 (100%) | | | | 15.0 (100%) |
| Services to property[3] | 18.4 (2%) | 679.0 (70%) | | 265.4 (28%) | 962.8 (100%) |
| Transportation | 93.8 (9%) | | | 956.6 (91%) | 1,050.4 (100%) |
| Welfare | 1.4 (100%) | | | | 1.4 (100%) |
| General management and support | 23.7 (99%) | | | 0.1 (1%) | 23.8 (100%) |
| Total | 308.0 (13%) | 810.7 (33%) | 31.7 (1%) | 1,276.4 (53%) | 2,426.8 (100%) |

[1]Includes contributions from adjacent municipalities.
[2]Includes some water/sewer; does not include CDBG funds.
[3]Includes fire, gas, water, and sewer.
*Source:* Philadelphia City Planning Commission, *1982/1987 Capital Program*, Philadelphia, 1982.

capital program are those requiring the smallest taxpayer contributions. All three of them—transportation, services to property, and economic development—are areas in which capital improvements are expected to promote economic development; they fall into the category of economic overhead capital (as opposed to social overhead capital). Pagano and Moore, in their study of capital budgeting in nine cities, identified a "profound philosophical shift that began in the mid-1970s," noting city officials' view that "the time had now come to refocus the city's activities on economic growth rather than on social programs."[12] Emphasizing officials' increased commitment to economic development, Pagano and Moore minimized the importance that local officials attached to the availability of federal grants when they decided how to divide tax dollars among different functional areas in the capital budget: "federal aid, as a variable that might affect city outlays on a particular function, will have a negligible impact."[13] However, they arrived at this conclusion by examining data for only two categories of capital expenditures (sewers and streets), showing that *within* each of these categories the year-to-year variation in local expenditures was not particularly responsive to changes in the level of federal subsidies for that category. They did not analyze the impact of federal subsidies on allocations among a wide range of expenditures, nor did they factor in any consideration of the self-sustaining nature of projects financed with revenue bonds.

Pagano and Moore are undoubtedly correct in identifying a philosophical shift in the 1970s toward greater concern for economic development as a goal of urban capital programs. This interpretation is confirmed by a HUD/National Science Foundation study of capital planning in eight cities that concluded that the basic objective of capital planners in "mature" cities like Philadelphia was to augment the tax base.[14] Yet the figures in table 6.2 strongly suggest that capital planners are at least as concerned about where the money comes from as they are about where it goes. Framers of the budget appear to put as much weight on how the expenditures will be financed as on what they will buy.

Table 6.2 also sheds some light on the difficulties that neighborhood activists and city council members face in trying to pressure budget makers to place greater emphasis on neighborhood services and less emphasis on citywide projects. The reasons for favoring highways, bridges, water treatment plants, stadiums, and convention centers are obvious. Economic development and services to property are both categories in which the ratio of self-sustaining debt to tax-supported debt is quite high. Because the city can issue revenue bonds to finance self-sustaining projects in virtually unlimited amounts, these categories will continue to be dominant in future capital programs. Similarly, so long as every tax dollar invested in transportation can leverage seven, eight, or even nine times its value in state and federal subsidies, this will probably remain the single biggest item in the capital program.

By contrast, the city's expenditures for health, welfare, recreation, housing, and law enforcement—those categories of most direct concern to communities—are financed primarily by tax-supported borrowing. These categories are therefore subject to the debt ceiling imposed by the state constitution. Traditionally, the city has maintained a policy of not borrowing all the way up to the state-imposed ceiling, in order to hold some of its borrowing power in reserve for emergencies. With the 1983–84 capital budget, however, the city reached the debt limit for the first time, giving officials no room to add more tax-supported projects without deleting others. Thus, the likelihood that more money can be included in future budgets for health, welfare, housing, law enforcement, and recreation facilities is exceedingly slim, although it is entirely possible to alter the distribution of these expenditures among categories.

Could user fees and charges be used to move at least some service facilities from the "tax-supported" to the "self-sustaining" column in the city's ledger? Inevitably, in the present period of austerity, increased attention is being focused on the role of such charges, which assess the cost of particular services to those who consume them. They can vary from special assessments to pay for sidewalks and street maintenance or water and sewer lines, to fees for fire protection, trash pickup, or the use of public swimming pools and tennis courts. Table 6.3 shows the growing reliance on user charges since 1970. One study of 300 American cities found that the revenue category showing the largest increases in the early 1980s was user charges, which jumped 15% in a single year.[15] By comparison with other large cities in the United States, Philadelphia does not rely very heavily on such fees and charges. In 1983–84, according to Census Bureau data, American cities with populations over 300,000 raised an average of 21% or their locally generated revenues from user charges, while Philadelphia raised only 13%.[16] A number of recent analyses of Philadelphia's budget problems have therefore suggested that the city begin to charge fees for more of its services.[17] For example, a proposal has been floated that would have the Free Library, the city's public library system, begin to charge for the privilege of borrowing books.

To make a significant contribution to the operating costs of community facilities as well as to debt service on their construction, user charges would have to be so high that their effect would be regressive. The city's low-and moderate-income residents would be hardest hit by such charges, both because they would find it harder to pay the fees and because they tend to rely more heavily on public services than do higher-income residents. So, while user charges are a well-established method of financing some public services, chiefly publicly provided utilities, their extension into other service areas must be evaluated cautiously.


## PHILADELPHIA'S EXPERIENCE MIRRORS NATIONAL TRENDS

We have seen that the trend of the last decade in financing Philadelphia's capital budget has brought an increase in the proportion of the budget that is classified as self-sustaining, and financed through revenue bonds. At the same time the proportion of the budget financed by tax-supported general obligation bonds has declined, as has the proportion supported by subsidies from higher levels of government. How closely does this trend parallel the experiences of the past decade in other American cities? Table 6.4 shows the change in the pattern of borrowing by state and local governments across the United States from 1950 to 1979. It documents a dramatic decline in the importance of general obligation bonds, which accounted for over 80% of all the outstanding long-term debt of state and local governments in 1950, but had dropped to only 28% of all debt by 1979. At the same

**Table 6.3**

Taxes and User Charges as Revenue Sources for American Cities, (in billions).

|  | *1971* | *1975* | *1979* |
|---|---|---|---|
| Taxes | $15.1 | $21.1 | $28.8 |
| User charges | 9.3 | 13.8 | 22.7 |
| Current charges | 3.6 | 5.4 | 8.8 |
| Utility revenue | 5.6 | 8.2 | 13.7 |
| Liquor store revenue | 0.1 | 0.2 | 0.2 |
| Ratio: Charges to $1 of taxes | 0.62 | 0.66 | 0.79 |

*Sources:* U.S. Bureau of Census, *City Government Finances*, annual issues.

time, the importance of revenue bonds rose sharply, especially during the 1970s.

A second parallel between Philadelphia's experience and national trends is the increasing tendency of facilities planners to "undershoot" their capital budgets. We noted in chapter 2 the widening gap during the 1970s between Philadelphia's capital budget, as passed by the city council, and the building program that actually followed from it. Many more projects have been written into the budget than can possibly be financed, and city officials treat the capital budget as a "wish list" from which they select certain proposals for implementation. There is evidence that cities across the country have experienced similar problems in following through on their capital spending plans. In 1981, for example, 300 cities included in a national study had realized, on average, only 60% of the spending which they had budgeted for capital.[18] Among the factors that reportedly accounted for this lag, the most important was financial—namely, the delay or cancellation of bond issues expected to finance the planned projects, mostly because of the high and rising interest rates. City governments were simply unwilling or unable to finance the debt service. Not surprisingly, the study found that general obligation bonds were more susceptible to delays and cancellations than were revenue bonds.

What parallels can we identify between the types of construction given priority in Philadelphia and in other cities? A recent survey of over 800 American city governments showed that the areas to which the respondents gave top priority were, in order: (1) streets and roads, (2) wastewater treatment, (3) storm water collection, and (4) sewers.[19] All of these fall into the category of citywide projects, a category that has accounted for larger and larger shares of Philadelphia's capital

**Table 6.4**

Long-Term Debt of American State and Local Governments, by Type of Issue, (in billions).

|  | 1950 | 1960 | 1970 | 1979 |
|---|---|---|---|---|
| General obligation bonds | $3.1 | $4.4 | $11.9 | $12.1 |
|  | (84%) | (69%) | (66%) | (28%) |
| Revenue bonds | .6 | 2.0 | 6.1 | 31.2 |
|  | (16%) | (31%) | (34%) | (72%) |

*Source:* John Petersen, "The Municipal Bond Market Heads in New Directions," *Urban Affairs Papers,* Vol. 2, No. 2, Spring 1980, p. 53.

program. Philadelphia is especially close to national trends in its emphasis in the 1970s on waste water treatment. In fact, the fastest growing segment of state and local capital expenditures in the mid-1970s was spending for municipal water treatment. As already mentioned, the priority accorded to this particular item came about as the result of federally imposed environmental standards, combined with a massive federal aid program to help bring cities into conformity with the new standards. Like the majority of capital aid programs, this one was not intended to provide any ongoing assistance to cities in operating the wastewater treatment facilities, but only to supply a one-time grant to assist with construction. In fact, the legislation included a stipulation that to be eligible for the construction grants, cities had to agree to impose user charges that would cover future operating costs and make the projects self-sustaining.[20]

The case of waste-water treatment serves to illustrate an important point about capital grants made to cities by the federal government. Despite the very high proportions of project cost these grants may cover (as much as 75%, and 90% in some cases), nevertheless they do not represent "free" money to the city. Whether the money goes for mass transit, public housing, or other types of facilities, Congress has historically preferred to limit its contribution to construction costs, leaving the cost of operating the new projects to local government. This limitation has been breached for certain programs in recent years (e.g., mass transit), but federal policy makers remain determined to minimize their support for operating expenses in order to force local governments to be self-reliant. So, for example, the Reagan administration began phasing out operating subsidies to mass transit, on the grounds that operating aid weakens local officials' incentives to keep costs down. In the end, the effect of federal capital assistance, like revenue bonds, is to increase the local taxpayers' burden in the form of user fees, rentals, and other types of charges to operate public facilities.


## ACCOUNTABILITY TO BONDHOLDERS VERSUS
## ACCOUNTABILITY TO CITIZENS


With the widespread stagnation of the tax bases of many large cities in the Northeast and Midwest, it seems reasonable to suppose that revenue bonds and federal aid will continue to have appeal for capital planners, despite the strings attached to them. Their use,

I have argued, tends to influence the types of projects likely to appear in capital programs. It also raises questions about whether a capital program that is based heavily on these types of financing mechanisms can possibly be responsive to neighborhood constituents, particularly those with low incomes.

As an illustration of this issue, let us look at a recent controversy in Philadelphia surrounding the Philadelphia Gas Works (PGW). PGW is a municipally owned utility that supplies natural gas to both homes and businesses in the city. It is an institution with a long and colorful history dating back to 1836. For most of the nineteenth century, the gas works was an important patronage haven and a political football. Because the gas works trustees controlled hundreds of jobs, some of them were able to exploit their control of the utility to gain substantial political power in the city. The leading example was "King" James McManes, a Republican ward leader who was appointed as a trustee in 1865. McManes used the position to consolidate his political power and to form an organization known as the "Gas Ring," which dominated Philadelphia politics for twenty-five years. In addition to controlling patronage jobs, the Gas Ring had a constant source of money in kickbacks paid by the coal suppliers who provided the gas works' fuel.[21] So powerful had McManes become that he was seen to control not just gas works jobs, but a large proportion of municipal employees as well. The Gas Ring trustees were finally ousted in a city charter reform in 1885, a move whose ultimate effect was not to eliminate graft but simply to transfer the benefits of graft from ward politicians to utility barons. In 1897 the city entered into a contract with the United Gas Improvement Company, operated by one such wealthy businessman, ignoring the loud protests of gas consumers.[22] Surprisingly, that arrangement remained in force for seventy-five years.

Finally, in 1972 the city changed the ordinance of PGW, instituting a dual control system that was intended to secure the best of both worlds for PGW: a nonprofit corporation to supply sound business management of the gas works, overseen by an appointed commission to insure that PGW remained responsive to the city's political leadership. Gas works employees belong to a separate union and receive a wage and benefit package separate from other city workers. And when the gas works issues bonds, its credit is not tied to that of the city's general government. Rather than being directly accountable to city government, PGW answers to the Philadelphia Gas Commission, composed of five members—two appointed by the mayor, two elected by the city council, plus the city controller—and acting as a kind of regulatory body, setting customer rates, approving both the capital and operating budgets, approving contracts, and setting standards for the gas works.

Yet the restructuring did not resolve the question of whether this municipally owned utility should be run as a business or used as an instrument of social and economic policy by the city. For example, industrial gas rates have periodically been lowered to persuade industrial users to stay in the city, in order to protect the job base. Certain groups of users have been given special rates; 84,000 elderly customers, for instance, were offered a 20% discount in 1978, which cost the company $5.4 million. On some occasions, especially during cold weather, the Gas Commission has issued moratoriums on shutoffs for customers with unpaid bills, in order to prevent serious public health problems. Neighborhood groups have protested shut-offs because they aggravate the shortage of low and moderately priced housing and encourage abandonment. Consumer advocacy groups, while they have supported these various concessions offered to consumers, have complained through Community Legal Services that the special programs have not been applied consistently, according to formalized policies and procedures.

Under increasing pressure to supply gas to people too poor to pay for it, PGW has introduced abatements, stretched-out payment programs, and numerous other devices to accommodate delinquent customers. The result is that PGW has the highest proportion of bad accounts of any gas utility in the country. In the average year PGW writes off about 5% of its sales as uncollectible, almost five times the proportion that is written off in New York, Boston, or Baltimore.

Still other groups within the community have advocated using PGW as the major instrument for energy conservation in Philadelphia. They were successful in the late 1970s in getting PGW to introduce a modest weatherization program for low-income homeowners which, by the end of 1981, had weatherized about 8,300 homes. On the basis of that demonstration, neighborhood groups and academics have urged PGW to undertake the massive task of insulating the city's entire housing stock.[23] It may at first seem odd to expect a company whose business is selling energy to take the major responsibility for such a conservation effort. But the plan's advocates point out that PGW possesses one key characteristic that equips it for this purpose— namely, its ability to borrow large amounts of capital through revenue bonds. The cost of a total residential conservation plan for the city amounts to several hundred million dollars, a sum that could only be considered reasonable if it were financed by bonds issued by a revenue-generating facility like PGW.

In early 1983, the tension between the view of PGW as a business and the view of PGW as an instrument of city policy came to a head. In January of that year, under a newly hired chief executive, PGW ended a moratorium it had been observing all winter on shut-offs, and began once again to send out termination notices to delinquent customers. The management of the gas works felt it could no longer survive under such a moratorium, given that the number of delinquent customers had increased from 64,000 to 146,000 over the previous three years, while accounts receivable had ballooned from $27.2 million to $95.5 million. Because of delinquencies and write-offs in 1982–83, cash-flow problems prompted Standard and Poor's rating service to downgrade the gas works' revenue bonds from A to A-, making them less attractive to investors. PGW's chief executive officer lamented that "We lost our A rating primarily due to delinquencies and the regulatory atmosphere in Philadelphia," a reference to the Gas Commission's refusal to allow PGW to deny service to delinquent customers, forcing the gas works to absorb the losses on delinquent accounts.[24]

Advocates of the elderly and the poor attacked the heartlessness of a municipal utility that would cut off heat and hot water in midwinter, and members of the city council began to consider ways to take the budgetary and rate-setting authority away from the Gas Commission and to place it instead in the city council. For the first time, the issue of whether PGW policies should be set by politicians or businessmen was openly debated in council hearings. One city council member expressed the legislators' desire for more direct control:

> We, the elected officials of Philadelphia, we're the ones people look to . . . I don't think the Gas Commission is adequately protecting the interests of the citizens, the customers, or the taxpayers.[25]

The council's opponents were equally adamant about leaving PGW in the hands of business management, overseen by the Gas Commission. The *Philadelphia Inquirer* editorialized that

> the quickest way to destroy the effectiveness of the Gas Works would be to turn it over to the City Council—lock, stock, and barrel—to become a perennial political football.[26]

If city council members think that PGW should be more closely controlled by the city government, attorneys representing the utility's low-income customers have taken the opposite position. Community Legal Services lawyers contend that PGW is too closely tied to city officials, particularly the mayor. Protesting against PGW's request for a rate increase of $59 million in 1986, the CLS attorneys argued that the Philadelphia Gas Commission, supposedly created to regulate rate increases, has an inherent conflict of interest. All five of its members, either directly or indirectly, represent the city government—a government that takes at least $18 million from PGW each year for the city's general fund. The availability of those funds, which can help to balance the budget or avert a tax increase, gives the mayor and council a stake in keeping gas revenues high. Hence, gas rates cannot be properly regulated by the politicians' representatives on the Gas Commission. At this writing, negotiations on a structural reorganization are stalled. But even if some structural changes are accepted by all parties, it will not resolve the most fundamental problem that arises from trying to use a facility like PGW to serve social ends.

As a capital-intensive operation, PGW must have constant access to large sums of money at reasonable interest rates. Policymaking for PGW must therefore be geared to insuring that the gas works continues to generate the revenues that are the basis for borrowing. So, for example, any large-scale weatherization program financed through revenue bonds must recover both the principal and the interest from the homeowners who benefit, making it unlikely to be affordable by those who most need it. The constraints imposed by the capital market make it extremely difficult to shape PGW policy to serve social ends. Granted, PGW officials have generally supported energy assistance programs for low-income customers, so long as they are financed from general tax revenues. But they have resisted manipulating PGW's own pricing policy to ease the burden on low-income customers, chiefly because their inability to recover costs ultimately jeopardizes their ability to borrow.[27]


## PUBLIC ACCOUNTABILITY AND INTERGOVERNMENTAL LINKS

Let us look briefly at one more example of a large-scale public works project in which the financial imperatives overwhelmed political debate. Only this time, the constraints on the city's options came from the state government rather than from the financial market. Planning for a new convention center, intended to be the largest public works project ever mounted in Philadelphia's history, occasioned both complex financial packaging and political maneuvering. In spring of 1982 a blue-ribbon steering committee made up of both government and corporate representatives began planning for a massive modern facility to supplant the city's outmoded exhibit hall. The city's economic planners, as well as the downtown business community, believed that such a facility would dramatically improve Philadelphia's appeal to convention planners, an appeal that was rapidly deteriorating as other cities rushed to build new centers.

It took a little over a year to select the downtown location and to design the financing arrangement for the $455 million project. The city's financial planners proposed a leasing arrangement in which the building would be constructed by a private investment group and then leased to the city under a thirty-year contract for payments of over a million dollars a month. Such arrangements have become increasingly popular with municipalities because they can secure capital facilities without issuing bonded debt. Since the city's monthly lease obligation is not considered to be "debt" in Pennsylvania, there is no requirement that voters approve such financing, nor does the construction cost count against the city's legal debt ceiling.[28]

Not all of the project cost, however, was to come from private investors. The city's plan required that the state government furnish $185 million for land acquisition and other project costs. When asked for the state's contribution, Pennsylvania's Republican governor surprised city officials by disapproving of a scheme that relied on private investors to build and own the convention center: "It would be inappropriate to permit private parties to derive substantial unearned profits from a project funded by hundreds of millions of public dollars."[29] The project, he insisted, must be publicly bid instead of built entirely by a single company, and it must be owned in the end by government instead of by private interests. (Political observers concluded that the governor's objection to the leaseback scheme was motivated, not by ideology, but by patronage considerations; a privately built center offered few opportunities to distribute jobs and contracts to the governor's political allies.) Months of negotiation finally ended in the city's capitulating to the governor's objections in order to secure the state money. The financial package was redesigned to eliminate the private investors' participation; the construction costs would be covered instead by bonds issued by a public authority set up to oversee the center.

Throughout the negotiations, neighborhood activists and members of the city council struggled to inject their concerns into the public debate. They worried about the thirty-year burden that this massive project would place on Philadelphia taxpayers for a facility that would probably remain vacant a good part of the year. That burden included not just the city's monthly lease payments but also all of the center's operating expenses (even the project's strongest backers admitted that convention centers operate at a loss, especially in the early years). Critics feared that the enormous center would become a white elephant. Several members of city council sought to insure that Philadelphia residents, especially minorities and women, would get a specified share of the jobs and contracts stemming from the massive construction project. State legislators representing the Philadelphia suburbs, on the other hand, were determined to block special hiring quotas because they might freeze out suburban workers and contractors. So heated was the contest for control over the project that at one point the president of city council threatened to withdraw the council's support for it because the city's negotiators were ceding too much ground to state officials. One council member representing North Philadelphia charged that "non-residents have controlled the whole thing from beginning to end." The Philadelphia Council of Neighborhood Organizations, representing 160 neighborhood groups, challenged the mayor's assertions about the benefits that the new convention center would bring for residents of the city's neighborhoods. The mayor's lobbyists in the state capitol were chagrined that the city was unable to present a united front. In the end the critics' tactics delayed, but did not prevent, the mayor from striking a bargain with the state.

Ultimately, the state government's control over its $185 million contribution to the project guaranteed its leverage on city officials. In exchange for the money, the state forced the city to establish a special-purpose authority to manage the project, almost half of whose members would be appointed by the state governor. The legislation creating the authority set up ground rules insisted upon by state Republicans for hiring personnel and letting contracts. What began as a municipal project had become a state/city project in which the city traded much of its control over management in order to secure critical funds.

## CONCLUSION

I have dwelt on the examples of the Philadelphia Gas Works and the proposed convention center because they illustrate only too well the difference between municipal policies that are based on responsiveness to funding sources and policies that are based on responsiveness to political constituents. Even if the city council were to gain direct control over both the gas works and the new convention center, would that insure that these enterprises would be operated to benefit the city's residents, especially low-income residents? Probably not, because the council would have to bow to the same financial realities.

As Philadelphia pushes against the constitutional ceiling on its indebtedness, municipal planners are seeking funds from sources other than tax-supported bonds. The limit on Philadelphia's bonded debt at any given time depends on the total value of the city's tax base, and in the 1980's that debt limit is rising more slowly than the city's need for capital. It is hardly surprising then that municipal officials are giving increasing attention to facilities that could be built using revenue bonds or leasing schemes in which the city's financial obligation takes the form of monthly lease payments to private interests. Nor is it surprising that the prospect of securing funds from state and federal sources would persuade Philadelphia officials to give up some control over capital projects. The result of bowing to these financial realities is that public works planners become less responsive to local political constituents when they make decisions such as choosing the kinds of facilities included in the capital program, awarding construction contracts, imposing affirmative action requirements on builders, levying user charges at finished facilities, and a variety of other operational issues.

# Conclusion

IN the introduction to this volume I described the efforts of several analysts to relate the economic decline and the accompanying fiscal strain experienced by many local governments to changes in their policy mix. One group of analysts, known as economic structuralists, has predicted that when cities face a declining market position, their political leaders are virtually forced to abandon redistributive expenditures. Urban administrators perceive programs that subsidize the disadvantaged at the expense of more affluent residents as undermining the city's competitive position. Hence, in times of economic decline local governments are likely to show an even more marked preference for developmental expenditures, defined as those that enhance the city's appeal to business.

How well do my findings bear out these predictions? The answer is that in general the Philadelphia case lends some support to the economic structuralists. In the 1970s, when Philadelphia's economic and fiscal position was declining, the priority in the city's capital program shifted dramatically toward the kind of major infrastructure systems that support economic activity, and away from facilities that serve neighborhood residents.

Table 7.1 shows how dramatic that shift was during the 1970s. It displays the Planning Commission's estimates of the balance between citywide and neighborhood projects in the capital programs adopted by the city since 1973. (Note that the figures in the table represent the capital programs as *proposed*, not necessarily as *completed*.) The trend is unmistakable: the city earmarked progressively smaller proportions of its total effort to neighborhood facilities. At the same time, there was a marked increase in the proportion of the capital program devoted to citywide projects. Note, however, that the increase does not necessarily represent a stepped-up commitment to downtown development, as many neighborhood advocates have assumed. Across the three mayoral administrations analyzed in chapter 6, the total commitment to center city projects remained quite stable. The really sharp rise came instead in the category of "Citywide Projects *not* located downtown," particularly infrastructure built to improve the city's water treatment and gas systems.

If Philadelphia's experience in the 1970s supports Paul Peterson's prediction that local governments faced with economic distress will show a strong preference for the category of policies that he calls "developmental," it does not necessarily confirm his corollary—i.e., that these same local governments will abandon redistributive expenditures. Nor does it support the variety of theories outlined in chapter 1, all of which assume that low-income and minority neighborhoods are likely to be underserved by public facilities. My analysis of spending patterns within the category of neighborhood facilities showed in fact a strong redistributive tendency. The picture that emerged from the Philadelphia data was not one of discrimination against poor or minority neighborhoods, in favor of more affluent

**Table 7.1**

Balance between Citywide and Neighborhood-Oriented Projects in Recent Capital Programs

|  | Citywide Projects | Neighborhood Projects |
|---|---|---|
| 1973–78 | 72% | 28% |
| 1974–79 | 73% | 27% |
| 1875–80 | 77% | 23% |
| 1976–81 | 84% | 16% |
| 1977–82 | 84% | 16% |
| 1978–83 | 87% | 13% |
| 1979–84 | 90% | 10% |
| 1980–85 | NA | NA |
| 1981–86 | 87% | 13% |
| 1982–87 | 91% | 9% |

*Source:* Philadelphia City Planning Commission, *Capital Programs* for the years given.

white neighborhoods. On the contrary, the poorest sections of North Philadelphia, West Philadelphia, and South Philadelphia received a disproportionately large share of the investments in community facilities during the thirty-year period under discussion. Particularly surprising was the finding that these neighborhoods received progressively larger shares of the funds spent on neighborhood projects in each successive decade, even while they suffered large population losses. How do we account for this unexpected conclusion? Does it mean that urbanists of various methodological schools have underestimated the political clout gained by disadvantaged groups during the past thirty years? I am dubious about that explanation; certainly the Philadelphia case does not support it. The disproportionate investments made in poor black neighborhoods, particularly in the 1970s, could hardly be seen as a display of their political influence; the well-known antagonism that existed between the Rizzo administration and these neighborhoods makes such an interpretation improbable. After all, the Rizzo administration had virtually no electoral debts in these areas. Nor is there much evidence that the city's poor neighborhoods exercised political power through the city council, which did not begin actively challenging the administration's capital programs until the late 1970s.

The favorable treatment shown by facility planners toward poor and minority areas of the city is attributable, I would argue, to a combination of factors having little to do with machine politics. The most important is that planners have used such facilities as part of their urban redevelopment strategy. In an earlier chapter I sketched the historical roots, within the Progressive movement, of the notion that the social reconstruction of lower-class communities can be accomplished through their physical rehabilitation. That faith in physical solutions to social problems was evident in the early postwar planning movement in Philadelphia, and later institutionalized in federal urban renewal legislation.

From the early renewal efforts of the 1950s, through the 1960 Comprehensive Plan, all the way through the Community Development Block Grant program of the 1970s and 1980s, Philadelphia's planning establishment has consistently viewed public services as a complement to, and a support for, housing improvements—a view that was strongly encouraged by federal programs. This role of public facilities as an element in the city's renewal strategy helps to account for the investment record in disadvantaged neighborhoods throughout the last several decades.

It does not necessarily explain why poor and minority neighborhoods were even more strongly favored in the 1970s than in previous decades. To understand why this trend accelerated in the 1970s, one needs to look at the way that austerity affected planners' choices of which projects to include in the annual budget. As the city's budgets grew tighter in the 1970s, the finance director was forced to be increasingly selective in choosing among the construction projects submitted each year by the various city departments. Department heads generally adopted a worst-first strategy in drafting their submissions, recognizing that the more they could convey a sense of urgency to the finance director and the Planning Commission, the better their chance of being included in the budget. The administration's shift in the 1970s toward a policy favoring expansion and rehabilitation of existing facilities over new construction, when combined with this tendency to spend limited resources on the worst cases first, led naturally to a spending pattern that favored older inner city neighborhoods.

The discovery that Philadelphia's disadvantaged areas have not suffered any marked discrimination in the allocation of community facilities is at odds with our on-the-ground observations about the city. If these areas have indeed received their share of public works, then why have they not benefited as expected? The answer seems to be that, contrary to the planners' expectations, the contribution made by neighborhood public improvements to the vitality of neighborhood housing markets is negligible.

Multivariate analysis showed the overwhelming importance of the residents' income level in predicting improvement or decline in neighborhood housing markets, but showed no association whatsoever between such housing changes and the amount of money invested in community facilities. Public investment neither led nor followed housing improvements over the thirty-year period; it was simply unrelated to housing shifts. While this finding conflicts with a number of empirical studies (mostly done in suburban settings) that have tied increases in public expenditures to increased housing values, it accords with survey data on residential mobility, which suggest that the presence of community facilities in a neighborhood does not influence the average household's choice of location.

In making their choices of what to build and where, how strongly influenced were capital planners by the city's business elite? Philadelphia entered the postwar era having the classic progrowth coalition at the helm of its urban renewal program. No one would dispute the power of business leaders over the planning agenda of the reform mayors; indeed, Mayor Richardson Dilworth was characterized as the businessman's "able servant."[1] But the political clout of this pro-growth coalition cannot by itself account for the pattern of public spending in the subsequent decades. For during the 1960s the administration of the machine-style mayor James Tate was far less aligned with the business community, and yet the proportion of Mayor Tate's capital program that went to center city projects and various citywide developmental projects was virtually the same as in the previous decade. (Refer to figure 6.1 in chapter 6.) Mayor Rizzo's administration in the 1970s did not close the gap between city government and the business community; if anything, that gap widened.

Doubtless some business executives did maintain direct links to government officials during the Tate and Rizzo years, despite the general climate of antagonism. As individuals, business people continued to serve on the boards of municipal authorities and commissions. But the evidence points to a marked decline in the participation of the city's corporate elite as an *organized* force in politics. By the early 1980s, corporate leaders themselves recognized that their efforts to influence city development policies had become fragmented and unfocused. Lamenting that they had lost the standing and confidence they had once enjoyed, they made a well-publicized effort to reestablish and rename the powerful Greater Philadelphia Movement, which had proven so effective in promoting business interests in the 1950s. Even with generous funding and an experienced professional staff, however, this new business coalition has not succeeded in reclaiming the role that organized business once played in Philadelphia.

The important point about this uneven record of business influence on city administrations is that it does not predict much about the pattern of capital spending. Even when the business community had no direct access to city hall, the capital budget favored large-scale, developmental projects. Indeed, the capital programs of the 1970s poured a steady stream of funds into center city projects and dramatically increased the emphasis on citywide development projects. The data recall to mind a question raised by Roger Friedland and William Bielby: "To what extent are policies produced which are beneficial to business without, or in spite of, their political participation?"[2]

If we are to understand the postwar pattern of capital spending, we need to look not just at the influence of business in city politics, but at the sources of funding for various kinds of projects. The shift away from neighborhood projects and toward citywide projects is a direct function of the difference in the availability of money for these two categories of facilities. The various types of neighborhood facilities contained in the city's capital program must be covered almost entirely by general tax revenues. The burden on the city treasury includes not only the cost of construction itself, but also the added operating costs of the new facility. In contrast, the development of the airport or port, of a convention center, of a sports stadium, or of the gas works, is likely to be financed through revenue bonds, which do not tap into the city's general revenues at all.

Other major citywide projects are eligible for massive federal subsidies. Interestingly, federal capital subsidies have been available to cities primarily for two types of projects that directly promote private economic development—highways and commercial redevelopment—while they have not been available for community facilities. The federal bias toward capital subsidies that promote economic development is surprising, since it might be presumed that these are precisely the kinds of projects that the private capital market would support without federal involvement. By maintaining this bias, Thomas Boast argues,

> The federal government—which could use a broader calculus than does the market in determining the need for subsidy or social reproduction uses—abdicated to the market the responsibility for these uses' financing. As a result, if a city was creating too many educational or health services or providing too many subsidies to particular sectors, the market could step in and call a halt. . . . Those cities that most successfully develop economic enterprises are rewarded with lower cost and more accessible market capital. Conversely, cities that pay for expanded public services with a declining tax base are penalized with higher market costs and less access.[3]

These financial facts of life make it difficult for capital planners not to emphasize projects that put the least strain on the city treasury. Nor should we expect this emphasis to change in the near future, given the city's continuing financial problems.

## AUSTERITY AND CENTRALIZATION

Applying economic structuralism to the politics of urban budgeting, Paul Kantor and Stephen David have argued that fiscal austerity and economic competition are likely to change the nature of the budgetary process by centralizing control within a narrowly defined elite. They reason that when a local government faces economic decline and fiscal stress, it will be forced to seek greater central coordination of the budget process. Its success in overcoming its market disadvantages will depend upon "the city's ability to close ranks in order to compensate for a weak negotiating position and to demonstrate the ability to implement budget objectives demanded by those outside of the city."[4] Does Philadelphia's experience support this picture of growing centralization and coordination of the budgetary process? Once again, the answer must be both yes and no.

It is true that control over the content and timing of the tax-supported portion of the capital program has shifted markedly during the 1970s toward the city administration and particularly toward the finance director's office. In this respect the capital program has become more centralized. We saw in chapter 2 that the trend in the capital program during the 1970s has been for the city council to appropriate far larger sums for projects than are subsequently spent. As the discrepancy grows between moneys appropriated and moneys spent, the discretionary power of city administrators grows proportionately.

Granted, it is the responsibility of the council and the electorate to approve the tax-supported bond issues that finance all approved projects. But even after the council and the voters have authorized bond issues, it is up to the city's finance director to decide when to issue the bonds. Furthermore, the authorization for a particular bond issue does not specify which projects are to be financed from its proceeds. Hence, the administration decides which construction expenditures are to be charged against a given issue. The combination of these powers to decide both when to issue new debt and which projects are to be charged against that debt gives city administrators very wide discretion in implementing the capital program. In recent years they have used that discretion to forestall some $150 million in new projects that had been included in capital budgets passed by the council but were never built.

Part of the explanation for the relative ease with which city administrators have appropriated more power in this process is the political disorganization that has characterized the city council. Although Democrats continue to dominate the council, as they have for the past thirty years in Philadelphia, the party has become more factionalized since 1970, with a particularly bitter split developing between the party regulars (many of whom are white ethnics) and the so-called new

Democrats (mainly blacks and white progressives). Without a well-organized party operating in the council, it has become increasingly difficult to engineer trade-offs within the legislative chamber; there are simply too many different agenda to be satisfied and no strong organization to broker the differences. The result in the case of the capital budget is that the council simply includes all members' submissions, making little effort to weed out the less urgent requests or to balance the additions in one category by deletions in other categories. Consequently, the job of making the painful choices among projects to be built falls to the city's chief administrators.

This situation is by no means unique to Philadelphia, nor am I the first to comment on its consequences. Theodore Lowi has written about the general shift of power in modern urban governments away from electoral organizations and toward professional bureaucracies, which Lowi calls "the new machine."[5] As authority has moved away from party leaders and toward bureaucratic professional elites, it has become possible for cities to be "well run but ungoverned," in the sense that government is unaccountable to any electorally based consensus. Looking more specifically at the effects of austerity on urban politics, Martin Shefter has written about New York City's fiscal crisis, drawing an intriguing contrast between the handling of that city's retrenchment in the 1970s and its earlier experience with the fiscal crisis of 1871. Shefter observes that New York's crisis in the 1970s led to centralization of authority in the hands of a small coalition of city administrators, bankers, and business representatives, whereas the fiscal crisis a hundred years earlier had been handled in the wider arena of electoral politics. The difference, Shefter points out, is that in the 1870s New York politics was structured by a

> political machine that exchanged patronage for votes, and had both a broad base and a centralized structure and was therefore able to subject voters, public officials, and public employees to its discipline. . . . Because politicians in New York today (in contrast to the situation during the heyday of Tammany rule) are independent political operators who are not subject to the discipline of a common party organization, the mayor and governor have found it difficult to compel other officials to pay heed to the imperatives imposed upon the city by the capital market.[6]

In summary, both the Philadelphia case and the New York City case appear to confirm Kantor and David's thesis, at least with regard to tax-supported expenditures. There *is* an observable tendency in periods of economic decline and fiscal austerity for budgetary authority to gravitate away from the legislative body and to become centralized in the hands of city administrators (who may, as in the New York City case, consult closely with bankers outside the administration). The explanation for this shift lies not only in the reason offered by Kantor and David (i.e., that the budget becomes a strategic planning tool). It occurs also because legislative bodies, particularly when they lack party discipline, have a difficult time making the cuts demanded by fiscal retrenchment.

## FRAGMENTATION OF SPECIAL-PURPOSE AUTHORITIES

At the same time this budgetary centralization is proceeding on one level, however, an equally important and opposing trend is occurring at another level. I refer to the increasing fragmentation of authority over the kinds of capital projects that are financed by revenue bonds as opposed to tax-supported bonds. Increasingly, large-scale development projects are planned and carried out by special authorities, operating authorities, public and quasipublic corporations that are independent of the city government. The establishment of such independent entities to oversee capital investment programs is a strategy that is now used in cities across the country, but it was pioneered in Philadelphia during the reform era of the 1950s. The first local example was the corporation established to organize and carry out the famous Greater Philadelphia Exhibition of 1947. Many others followed as vehicles for the reformers' redevelopment campaign, including the Food Distribution Center Corporation, which built a massive modern facility to house the city's wholesale food trade, the Philadelphia Industrial Development Corporation to lure new industrial firms to the area, the Old Philadelphia Development Corporation to redevelop Philadelphia's historic central district, and the Philadelphia Housing Development Corporation to help build low-cost housing. Histories of the reform period suggest that these quasipublic corporations were established as natural extensions of the close corporate/governmental links that distinguished the entire reform movement: "The institution of the quasi-public corporation implied a relation of trust between the public and civic or business groups for jointly pursuing the public purpose."[7] Whether they were labeled corporations or authorities, the organizational model remained substantially the same; they were typically overseen by boards of directors including representatives of both private capital and the public sector. Most often, financial sponsorship was shared between the public and private sectors, and occasionally also involved federal funds.

What is the advantage to the city of creating a multitude of independent corporations to implement the city's physical redevelopment? The most common justification for putting major capital investment programs into the hands of such corporations is of course that they will be more likely to undertake their mission in a businesslike manner if they are operated independently of the political process. Having no direct political accountability, their managers are free to use pure efficiency criteria to make operating decisions. Typically, civil service protections do not extend to employees of these independent authorities, giving management more flexibility in hiring, promoting, or firing staff. And the clarity of their mission, when compared with the complex functions performed by general-purpose government, makes it easier to evaluate their performance.[8]

In recent years a second kind of advantage enjoyed by these quasipublic entities has become an even more compelling argument for their proliferation: they make it easier to obtain financing for development projects. As we saw in chapter 6, Philadelphia and other cities are turning increasingly to the device of revenue bonds to expand their development activities beyond those that can be supported solely from tax revenues. The requirement that any project funded by revenue bonds be absolutely self-supporting makes the independent corporation or the independent authority a natural vehicle for overseeing such an undertaking, particularly if it is a large-scale project with long-term debt. Independent authorities can borrow for large projects without having the debt count against the municipality's total indebtedness. Thus they are an especially attractive option for cities approaching the legal limit of their debt. Moreover, public authorities can borrow money without going to voters for a referendum, and thus are not vulnerable to taxpayer revolts. They make it possible to circumvent both constitutional and political limits on capital spending. As a consequence, we will continue to see a large proportion of the city's capital program managed outside the bounds of electoral politics.

Philadelphia is by no means unique in these developments. Local governments across the country have increasingly resorted to independent corporations and authorities to manage capital investments. A recent study documented the extent of this practice, which the authors labeled "off-budget spending and borrowing"—a reference to the fact that these independent bodies fall outside of the control of elected government. Noting that Pennsylvania is by far the most active state in the union in the level of off-budget spending and borrowing at the local level, the study showed that other states are rapidly following Pennsylvania's lead.[9]

This proliferation of autonomous agencies engaged in development planning is troubling to those on both the political right and left. An example of criticism from the libertarian viewpoint is the Cato Institute's critique entitled *Underground Government*. Its message is simple: irresponsible government officials, intent upon enlarging the scope of the public sector against the wishes of taxpayers, are using various off-budget agencies to evade limits on public spending: "The historical record reveals that the primary attraction of off-budget entities was the evasion of restrictive limitations on government borrowing."[10] The study highlights the federal government's role, beginning in the 1930s, in encouraging the concept as a way to promote public works as a stimulant to the depressed economy. Both the Reconstruction Finance Corporation and the Public Works Administration in effect subsidized development authorities by purchasing their revenue bonds. Since the 1930s dozens of federal programs (including public housing, public facilities loans, and hospital construction) have called for the creation of special local authorities to float bonds and to oversee construction projects. The massive resources at the disposal of all these nongovernmental units, according to the study's authors, is a clear sign that big government is out of control.

Interestingly, some of the same criticisms are offered by leftist critics. Roger Friedland, Frances Piven, and Robert Alford have argued that in its role as handmaiden to economic elites, local government must insure that its support for capital accumulation is not jeopardized by popular protests. Hence it creates special authorities outside the reach of normal political processes:

> To assure that urban governments are responsive to the requirements of accumulation, agencies charged with its management are institutionalized beyond popular or political control.[11]

Thus, what appears to be a technical and legal justification for separate authorities to manage discrete projects in a financially responsible way is interpreted by these critics as a thinly disguised strategy of political domination. Whereas the libertarian critique sees these off-budget operations as an extension of overly ambitious governments, Friedland et al. see them as yet another sign of the captive status of local government vis-à-vis economic elites.

However one chooses to interpret the motivations behind the creation of these autonomous bodies, it is clear that they will continue to proliferate, especially in times of fiscal retrenchment when local tax bases are incapable of fully supporting the cities' capital needs. That means that the financing for a significant portion of Philadelphia's infrastructure will continue to be managed by nongovernmental agencies—hardly a sign that budgetary control is being centralized, as Kantor and David have predicted.

The fragmentation of authority and direction in the city's infrastructure management makes it difficult to implement a coordinated development strategy, and the problem is even more acute for a city like Philadelphia whose political leadership is fragmented as well.

> City government, when internally divided, is in a weak position even to negotiate with individual authority boards, each of which has a relatively clear idea of its mission, a fairly straightforward calculus for achieving it, and an insulation from the public that frees it from worrying about citizen input or hostile interests groups.[12]

Not only coordination, but also compromise, is made more difficult by the proliferation of single-function authorities. City officials have very little opportunity to redistribute resources among uses, functions, projects, etc., when the management of infrastructure is divided among so many separate bodies, each of which is responsive to its own bondholders. Trade-offs are far more difficult to engineer than in a unified system.


## TWO CAPITAL BUDGETS

In this chapter we have examined two hypotheses regarding the effects of fiscal austerity on local government budgets: the first hypothesis predicted that austerity brings with it a shift away from redistributive expenditures and toward developmental expenditures, and the second predicted that austerity leads to increased centralization in the budgetary process. In both cases, Philadelphia's experience with capital budgeting partially confirmed, but also partially disconfirmed the hypothesis. The fiscal squeeze of the 1970s led to a discernible emphasis on development projects, but also to an accelerated redistribution of resources within the category of neighborhood facilities. It led to centralization in the process by which tax-supported projects are budgeted, but to a simultaneous fragmentation of budgetary authority for development that is financed by revenue bonds.

How do we explain these mixed findings? The answer is that Philadelphia does not have a single capital budget, but rather two distinct capital budgets whose operation and outcomes must be analyzed separately. What distinguishes the two budgets is the source of revenues supporting them. And although they are annually presented in a single capital program document as if they constituted a single budget, they do not. There is first the package of projects supported from the city's tax base; it is invariably the primary subject of interest in the city council's annual hearings on the capital budget. While a great deal of heated debate ensues in council about the relative merits of one library, swimming pool, or skating rink over another, the reality of recent years has been that it is city bureaucrats and not the council that finally establishes the priority among projects. This process of priority setting has had redistributive results, with poor and minority neighborhoods being favored over wealthier white sections of the city.

The city's second capital budget is the collection of projects financed primarily off-budget by revenue bonds or intergovernmental grants or a combination of the two. Such projects do not normally compete for funds with those in the tax-supported budget; they constitute an entirely separate category of expenditures. They are usually supported by a well-financed coalition of developers and business interests; what opposition exists comes from residents or business people who may be displaced by new construction. But because developmental projects can be sold to the public as contributors to the local economy, and because the money need not come from the coffers of city government, to oppose them is tantamount to opposing civic progress. Once approved, these projects are most often managed outside the city government, much the same way that any business manager would operate. While a publicly owned investment need not generate profits, and usually enjoys tax concessions not available to private enterprise, nevertheless the responsibility of the city to its creditors imposes constraints on public managers that are similar to those faced by management in the private sector. They must obtain a sufficient return on the investment through rentals, user fees, or other methods, to redeem their outstanding debt. This overriding obligation to their bondholders, rather than to the urban electorate, leaves them little room to shape their operating policies in ways that advance the public welfare.

The classic example is the case of the Philadelphia Gas Works described in chapter 6. The management of the gas works has insisted that the utility be operated according to accepted business practices, charging a reasonable fee for its product and avoiding the temptation to manipulate pricing policies for social ends. This viewpoint has been challenged by interests in the community which see the gas works as a publicly owned asset whose management should be accountable to the publicly elected government of the city.

## HOW IMPORTANT IS LOCAL POLITICS?

The classical pork-barrel model of urban public works interprets capital items as rewards doled out to electoral constituents in order to secure votes. A recent analysis of Cleveland's capital spending, for example, concluded that neighborhood improvements have continued to be funded there, at the expense of citywide projects, precisely because the neighborhood improvements buy votes while the citywide projects do not. Focusing primarily on Cleveland's city council as the arena for political dealing on the capital budget, the author concluded that the chronic underinvestment in the city's water lines and other large capital systems is "the natural failing of a system that concentrated on local improvements at the expense of broader concerns."[13] This is an explanation that relies on local politics as the primary determinant of capital spending patterns.

My interpretation, on the other hand, stresses the overwhelming importance of the city's access to outside resources as the key to its development policies. I have laid particular emphasis on access to the capital market as paramount in determining what projects are built and how they are to be operated. The market's demand for a secure return on investments has encouraged the city to establish an array of public authorities and corporations to manage these enterprises outside of the political domain. To assert the determinative influence of capital sources as the key to development patterns is to suggest that even if the so-called progrowth coalition is supplanted by proneighborhood forces in city politics, the bias in the city's development program is likely to change only marginally. Neighborhood advocates find themselves operating in precisely the same capital market as any other group of decision makers and encounter the same difficulties in raising money. Like any other group of public planners, they have a far easier time obtaining capital to build revenue-producing facilities than other kinds of projects.

It would be going too far to conclude that local politics makes no difference at all. My analysis suggests, however, that political organizers find it far more difficult to influence the city's large-scale capital developments than the projects financed by local tax revenues. In the allocation of local tax dollars, the interplay between the city council, the mayor and the professional bureaucracy, neighborhood and business groups determines the outcomes. Here, there *are* choices available to the city as to how its money is spent, and these choices are shaped by the configuration of local politics. For example, the political disarray within the city's Democratic party has had the effect of shifting more authority for locally financed projects into the hands of the city's chief administrators. The absence of a strong political party organization makes it difficult for elected officials to play the brokering role that they would need to play in order to control spending priorities within the second capital budget. A strong party organization would be able to impose the discipline required to choose among competing projects. It could make sure that neighborhoods suffering cutbacks in certain categories of facilities were compensated in other ways.

Even without a strong party organization, however, it is still possible for well-organized communities to halt projects that threaten their neighborhoods. Particularly when such projects pose environmental or public health hazards, neighborhood associations may be able to strengthen their protests by aligning themselves with environmentalists.[14] One recent instance of such a protest came from residents in South Philadelphia who opposed the city's plan to build in their neighborhood a major new incinerator to burn trash and recover energy in the form of steam heat. Their main objection was its potential for emitting dangerous cancer-causing chemicals into the air, but they protested as well against the damaging effects of traffic congestion and foul odors associated with the plant's operation. By aligning themselves with liberal environmentalists across the city, this working-class neighborhood has successfully stalled the plant's construction for over five years, despite heavy pressure from the business community.

Although it is easy to find examples of communities in Philadelphia and elsewhere that successfully organized to stop a particular construction project in their midst, it is far more difficult to identify instances in which neighborhood residents mobilized successfully to build or rebuild housing and community facilities. That is because building such structures often depends not on traditional political strategies, but on new modes of organization that allow neighborhoods to tap the sources of private finance capital.

The track record of neighborhood groups working directly with developers and financial institutions is not a long one, and it is a record of mixed results. The burgeoning of community development corporations in cities across the country shows that community activists have recognized the importance of organizing to work with private sector actors as well as with their more traditional partners in government. Especially since 1980, federal policy has pushed neighborhood groups in this direction by relying more on investment tax credits and private market strategies, while cutting direct subsidies to neighborhood development. And while the federal government's emphasis on public-private partnerships has spawned a great deal of innovation in development financing, we must recognize the limitations inherent in this new policy approach.

Gone are the days of large-scale federal urban renewal programs, public housing programs, and other city building programs that relied on federal grants. The new emphasis in federal policy is to encourage cities to seek investment funds from private sources for housing rehabilitation, community facilities, downtown renovations, and a host of public facilities. Cities like Philadelphia have even considered turning to private investors to finance their prisons and municipal office buildings. Observers of this trend in capital financing, labeled "privatization," have sometimes mistakenly assumed that it represents a withdrawal of federal subsidies from urban development. It does not. It constitutes a change in the form of federal subsidy, away from direct grants and toward tax expenditures.

In most public-private development schemes the federal treasury remains an important source of subsidies, but those subsidies take the form of tax concessions for investors rather than direct grants to development agencies. The federal government is a silent partner in every development project that benefits investors through tax-exemption on industrial revenue bonds or mortgage revenue bonds, historic preservation tax credits, depreciation allowances on income-producing properties, whether they be rental housing, stadiums, exhibit halls, or even municipal office buildings. And increasingly, municipal officials and neighborhood activists are relying on such tax concessions to secure private capital to build public facilities.

It is easy to see why federal policy makers are attracted to the idea of substituting tax concessions for the direct grants that once went to urban redevelopment agencies. On one hand, some legislators who are critical of the cities' performance in urban renewal programs see subsidies to private investors as a more efficient use of public resources than putting money into the hands of wasteful municipal bureaucrats. On the other hand, legislators who are more sympathetic to urban governments see tax concessions as an easier form of subsidy to provide than grants, because the cost is less visible to the media and the public. In an era of fiscal conservatism in government, it is more difficult to justify spending tax dollars than it is to forego collecting them in the first place. And while Congress reduced the level of concessions for development in the 1986 Tax Reform Act, tax incentives still remain the most important federal vehicle for subsidizing the renewal and development of the urban infrastructure.

This Philadelphia case study sounds a cautionary note for those who would see public-private partnerships as a substitute for more traditional tax-funded public works. Clearly, in order for tax concessions to draw more private capital into public works, the projects must generate returns for investors. As we have seen, this simple fact may seriously distort a community's development agenda. Projects of secondary importance may get priority, while more critical needs go unmet because they are not sufficiently enticing to private investors.

My research suggests that local voters already have difficulty exercising democratic control over large portions of the municipal capital budget. Continuing privatization of public works will only weaken local political accountability further. It is not that this policy of privatization removes development financing from the political arena altogether. In fact, Congress exerts a powerful influence over developmental patterns by its manipulation of the tax code. (For example, tax policies were crucial in fostering the boom in office construction in the early 1980s). But to employ federal tax incentives as the primary instrument of policy is to locate the political debate at the national level, beyond the reach of local constituencies. The fundamental political choices about which types of development gain the benefit of public subsidy are made by Congress and the Internal Revenue Service, rather than by mayors, city councils, or local development agencies.

Ironically, the political conservatives in Washington who have led the campaign to reduce direct grants to cities in favor of more market-oriented approaches are the very same conservatives who urge stronger local democracy as a counterbalance to an overly powerful central government. My study suggests that in the matter of financing public works, these two goals are not entirely compatible. Indeed, federal policy makers may end up achieving their first goal only at the expense of their second.

# *Appendix 1*

Breakdown of Capital Programs for 1954–59, 1966–71, 1974–79

**Table 1.A.**

Capital Expenditures for Neighborhood Facilities, (in millions of dollars)*.

|  | 1954–59 | 1966–71 | 1974–79 |
|---|---|---|---|
| Urban renewal | $24.7 | $22.5 | $17.1 |
| Mass transit | 8.8 | .4 | — |
| Major roads | 25.5 | 35.6 | 3.4 |
| Bridges | 3.8 | 6.8 | 1.0 |
| Parking | — | 0.4 | — |
| Garages, service, and storage facilities | 2.3 | 3.2 | 0.7 |
| Fire stations | 4.4 | 2.3 | 1.6 |
| Police stations | 3.5 | 1.6 | 0.2 |
| Water/sewer | 32.5 | 6.3 | 4.7 |
| Storm flood relief | 15.9 | — | — |
| Parks/recreation | 19.7 | 21.7 | 13.3 |
| Libraries | 2.0 | 3.9 | 3.6 |
| Neighborhood museum | — | — | 0.8 |
| Health centers | 2.4 | 1.6 | 1.0 |
| Totals | $118.9 | $106.2 | $47.6 |

*Dollars adjusted to 1967 values.

**Table 1.B.**
Capital Expenditures on Center City Projects, (in millions of dollars)*.

| | 1954–59 | 1966–71 | 1974–79 |
|---|---|---|---|
| City hall | $1.9 | $11.7 | $3.1 |
| Downtown redevelopment | 0.6 | 8.7 | 5.5 |
| Tourism center | 0.1 | — | — |
| Mass transit | 2.1 | 5.9 | 10.2 |
| Major roadways | 26.9 | 7.1 | 0.8 |
| Bridges | — | 0.3 | — |
| Parking | — | 3.7 | — |
| Heliport | — | 0.1 | — |
| Police administration buildings | 4.6 | 0.5 | 0.3 |
| Fire administration buildings | — | — | 2.3 |
| Municipal services buildings | — | 0.1 | — |
| Museums | 1.3 | 1.2 | 11.8 |
| Urban beautification | — | 0.3 | — |
| Historic restoration | — | — | 0.9 |
| Fairmount Park | 2.1 | 2.9 | 8.4 |
| Penn's Landing | — | 0.1 | — |
| Downtown recreation | 0.2 | 0.8 | 0.8 |
| Library | 0.2 | 0.1 | — |
| Health center | 2.6 | — | — |
| Totals | $42.4 | $43.7 | $44.2 |

*Dollars adjusted to 1967 values.

**Table 1.C.**
Capital Expenditures on Citywide Facilities *Not* Located Downtown, (in millions of dollars)*.

|  | 1954–59 | 1966–71 | 1974–79 |
|---|---|---|---|
| Airports | 32.2 | $25.1 | $31.6 |
| Port | 4.2 | 13.7 | 3.7 |
| Bridges | 26.5 | 12.1 | 5.9 |
| Major expressways | 28.7 | — | 28.5 |
| Food distribution center | 9.4 | 2.5 | — |
| Civic center | 4.1 | 19.3 | 9.5 |
| Gas works | 11.5 | 25.4 | 46.0 |
| Incinerators | 14.0 | 4.2 | 3.1 |
| Water treatment plants | 42.7 | 14.1 | 91.0 |
| Water pumping stations | 11.9 | 11.2 | 3.8 |
| Storage yards | 0.3 | 0.3 | — |
| Citywide recreation | 0.6 | 35.2 | — |
| Municipal hospital | 9.1 | 18.4 | 0.1 |
| Correctional facilities | 2.1 | 0.9 | 3.4 |
| Homes for aging | 3.3 | 2.2 | 0.6 |
| Child welfare center | 1.8 | — | — |
| Fireboat, training stations | — | 0.2 | 1.0 |
| Totals | $203.3 | $185.3 | $228.3 |

*Dollars adjusted to 1967 values.

# *Appendix 2*

# *Notes*

## CHAPTER 1

1. John Mollenkopf, *The Contested City* (Princeton: Princeton University Press, 1983); Susan Fainstein, Norman Fainstein, Richard Child Hill, Dennis Judd, and Michael Peter Smith, *Restructuring the City: The Political Economy of Urban Development*, 2nd ed. (New York: Longman, 1986).

2. Edgar Hoover and Raymond Vernon, *Anatomy of a Metropolis* (Cambridge, Mass.: Harvard University Press, 1959).

3. David Birch, "Toward a Stage Theory of Urban Growth," *American Institute of Planners Journal* (1971) pp. 78–87.

4. Public Affairs Counseling, "The Dynamics of Neighborhood Change" (prepared under contract for U.S. Department of HUD, Office of Policy Development and Research, Washington, DC, 1975).

5. David Harvey, "The Urban Process Under Capitalism: A Framework for Analysis," *International Journal of Urban and Regional Research* (1978) pp. 101–131.

6. Arthur Naparstek and Gale Cincotta, *Urban Disinvestment: New Implications for Community Organization. Research and Public Policy* (Washington, DC: National Center for Urban Ethnic Affairs, 1976).

7. Neil Smith, "Toward a Theory of Gentrification," in Robert Lake, ed., *Readings in Urban Analysis* (New Brunswick, NJ: Rutgers University Center for Urban Policy Research, 1983), pp. 278–98.

8. Pat Choate and Susan Walter, *America in Ruins: Beyond the Public Works Pork Barrel* (Washington, DC: Council of State Planning Agencies, 1981), p. 17.

9. Exceptions to this generalization are: the American Society of Planning Officials' study of capital planning in eight communities, reported in Frank So, Michael Meshenberg, and Judith Getzels, *Local Capital Improvements and Development Management: Literature Synthesis* (Chicago: American Society of

Planning Officials, 1977); Margaret Corwin and Judith Getzels, "Capital Expenditures: Causes and Controls," in Robert Burchell and David Listokin, eds., *Cities Under Stress: The Fiscal Crisis of Urban America* (New Brunswick, NJ: Rutgers University Center for Urban Policy Research, 1981), pp. 387–400; and the multicity project undertaken in the late 1970s by the Urban Institute which produced six separate volumes dealing with the capital programs of New York, Cleveland, Cincinnati, Dallas, Oakland, and Boston, all published by the Urban Institute between 1979 and 1981. The ASPO study cited above investigated whether communities actually made expenditures in accordance with their stated development plans, while the Urban Institute project concentrated mainly on the impact of the six cities' financial problems on their capital and maintenance programs.

10. This distinction is developed by Niles Hansen in "The Structure and Determinants of Local Public Investment Expenditures" *Review of Economics and Statistics* 47 (1965) pp. 150–62.

11. John Mollenkopf, "Paths Toward the Post Industrial Service City: The Northeast and the Southwest," in Burchell and Listokin, *Cities Under Stress*, p. 108.

12. Manuel Castells, *The Urban Question: A Marxist Approach* (Cambridge, Mass.: MIT Press, 1977).

13. Daniel Fusfeld, *The Basic Economics of the Urban Racial Crisis* (New York: Holt, Rinehart, Winston, 1973), p. 43.

14. Astrid Merget, "Achieving Equity in an Era of Fiscal Constraint," in Burchell and Listokin, *Cities Under Stress*, pp. 401–36.

15. Bernard Frieden and Marshall Kaplan, "Community Development and the Model Cities Legacy," Working Paper No. 42 (Joint Center for Urban Studies of the MIT and Harvard University, Boston, 1976) pp. 4–5.

16. For summaries of this new school see Harvey Boulay, "Social Control Theories of Urban Politics," *Social Science Quarterly* 59, no. 4 (March 1979) pp. 605–21; Norman and Susan Fainstein, "New Debates in Urban Planning: The Impact of Marxist Theory within the U.S.," *International Journal of Urban and Regional Research* 3, no. 3 (1979) pp. 381–403; John Walton "Urban Political Economy: A New Paradigm," *Comparative Urban Research* 7, no. 1 (1979) pp. 5–17. For bibliography, see C. Hoch and J. Friedman, *Radical Urban Political Economy: A Bibliographic Introduction*, Public Administration Series Bibliography P–442 (Monticello, Ill.: Council of Planning Librarians, 1980).

17. Larry Sawers, "New Perspectives on the Urban Political Economy," in William Tabb and Larry Sawers, eds., *Marxism and the Metropolis*, 2d. ed. (New York: Oxford University Press, 1984), p. 6.

18. James O'Connor, *The Fiscal Crisis of the State* (New York: St. Martin's Press, 1973), p. 105.

19. Richard Peet, "Inequality and Poverty: A Marxist-Geographic Theory" *Annals of the Association of American Geographers* 65, no. 4 (December 1975) p. 570.

20. Kirk Petshek, *The Challenge of Urban Reform* (Philadelphia: Temple University Press, 1973), pp. 138ff.

21. Anthony Downs, "Using the Lessons of Experience to Allocate Resources in the Community Development Program," in *Recommendations for Community Development Planning* (Chicago: Real Estate Research Corporation, 1976).

22. Richard Nathan, Paul Dommel, Sarah Liebshutz, Milton Morris and Associates, *Block Grants for Community Development* (Washington, DC: Brookings Institution, January 1977), pp. 329–31. See also Donald Strickland and Dennis Judd, "Capital Investment in Neighborhoods: Theories which Inform National Urban Policy in the U.S.," *Population Research and Policy Review* 1, no. 1 (1982) pp. 59–78.

23. Frank Levy, Arnold Meltsner and Aaron Wildavsky, *Urban Outcomes: Schools, Streets, and Libraries* (Berkeley: University of California Press, 1974).

24. Robert Lineberry, *Equality and Urban Policy: The Distribution of Municipal Public Services* (Beverly Hills: Sage, 1977).

25. Bryan Jones, Saadia Greenberg and Joseph Drew, *Service Delivery in the City: Citizen Demand and Bureaucratic Rules* (New York: Longman, 1980).

26. Kenneth Mladenka, "The Urban Bureaucracy and the Chicago Political Machine: Who Gets What and the Limits of Political Control," *American Political Science Review* 74, no. 4 (December 1980) pp. 991–8. Mladenka's findings have been reexamined and his conclusions challenged in David Koehler and Margaret Wrightson, "Inequality in the Delivery of Urban Services: A Reconsideration of the Chicago Parks," *Journal of Politics* (February 1987) pp. 80–99.

27. John Boyle and David Jacobs, "The Intracity Distribution of Services: A Multivariate Analysis," *American Political Science Review* 76, no. 2 (June 1982) pp. 371–9.

28. Fredric Bolotin and David Cingranelli, "Equity and Urban Policy: The Underclass Hypothesis Revisited," *Journal of Politics* (February 1983) pp. 209–19.

29. Richard Rich, "Distribution of Services: Studying the Products of Urban Policymaking," in Dale Marshall, ed., *Urban Policy Making* (Beverly Hills: Sage, 1979), p. 239.

30. J. Little, "Residential Preferences, Neighborhood Filtering, and Neighborhood Change," *Journal of Urban Economics* 13, no. 1 (January 1976) pp. 68–81; Jonathan Marks, Thomas Boehm and Charles Leven, "A Probability Model for Analyzing Interneighborhood Mobility," in David Segal, ed., *The Economics of Neighborhood* (New York: Academic Press, 1979); Thomas Boehm and Jonathan Mark, "A Principal Component Logistic Analysis of the Mobility Decision in Transitional Neighborhoods," *Journal of the American Real Estate and Urban Economics Association* 8, no. 3 (1980) pp. 299–319.

31. William Grigsby, Louis Rosenberg, Michael Stegman and James Taylor, *Housing and Poverty* (Philadelphia: University of Pennsylvania Institute for Environmental Studies, 1971).

32. Rolf Goetze, *Neighborhood Monitoring and Analysis: A New Way of Looking at Urban Neighborhoods and How They Change.* (U.S. Department of HUD, Office of Policy Development and Research, Washington, DC, June 1980) pp. 12–13.

33. Ibid., p. 14.

34. Mark LaGory and John Pipkin, *Urban Social Space* (Belmont, California: Wadsworth Pub. Co., 1981), p. 149.

35. Peter Rossi, *Why Families Move* (Glencoe, Ill., Free Press, 1955); William Michelson, *Environmental Choice, Human Behavior, and Residential Satisfaction* (New York: Oxford University Press, 1977); W. A. V. Clark and Eric Moore, eds., *Residential Mobility and Public Policy* (Beverly Hills: Sage, 1980).

36. Michael Gleeson, *Urban Growth Management Systems: An Evaluation of Policy-Related Research*, Planning Advisory Service Report Nos. 309–10 (Chicago: American Society of Planning Officials, August 1975).

37. David Godschalk, David Brower, Larry McBennett, and Barbara Vestl, *Constitutional Issues of Growth Management* (Chicago: American Society of Planning Officials, 1977).

38. So, Meshenberg and Getzels, *Local Capital Improvements*, p. 38.

39. Philadelphia City Planning Commission, *Comprehensive Plan: A Physical Development Plan for the City of Philadelphia*, (Philadelphia, 1960).

40. Aaron Wildavsky, *The Politics of the Budgetary Process* (Boston: Little, Brown and Co., 1964), p. 4.

41. Michael Lipsky, *Street-Level Bureaucracy* (New York: Russell Sage Foundation, 1980).

42. Lineberry, *Equality and Urban Policy*, p. 154.

43. Michael Pagano and Richard Moore, *Cities and Fiscal Choices: A New Model of Urban Public Investment* (Durham: Duke University Press, 1985), p. 50.

44. Ibid., p. 97.

45. John Logan and Harvey Molotch, *Urban Fortunes: The Political Economy of Place* (Berkeley: University of California Press, 1987); John Mollenkopf, *The Contested City* (Princeton: Princeton University Press, 1983); Robert Salisbury, "The New Convergence of Power in Urban Politics," *Journal of Politics* (November 1964) pp. 775–97.

46. Chester Hartman, *The Transformation of San Francisco* (Totowa, NJ: Rowman and Allanheld, 1984).

47. Amy Klobuchar, *Uncovering the Dome* (Prospect Heights, Ill.: Waveland Press, 1986).

48. Roger Friedland and Donald Palmer, "Park Place and Main Street: Business and the Urban Power Structure," *Annual Review of Sociology* 10 (1984) pp. 393–416.

49. Todd Swanstrom, "Urban Populism, Fiscal Crisis, and the New Political Economy," in Mark Gottdiener, ed., *Cities in Stress* (Beverly Hills: Sage Publications, 1986), p. 82.

50. Paul Peterson, *City Limits* (Chicago: University of Chicago Press, 1981), p. 4.


## CHAPTER 2


1. Edward Teitelman and Richard Longstreth, *Architecture in Philadelphia: A Guide* (Cambridge, Mass: MIT Press, 1974), p. 2.

2. W. H. Brown and C. E. Gilbert, *Planning Municipal Investment: A Case Study of Philadelphia* (Philadelphia: University of Pennsylvania Press, 1961), p. 13.

3. Jeanne Lowe, *Cities in a Race with Time: Progress and Poverty in America's Renewing Cities* (New York: Random House, 1967), p. 313.

4. Dennis Clark, *The Urban Ordeal: Reform and Policy in Philadelphia, 1947 to 1967* (University of Pennsylvania, Center for Philadelphia Studies, 1982) p. 4.

5. Kirk Petshek, *The Challenge of Urban Reform* (Philadelphia: Temple University Press, 1973), pp. 18–19. Petshek was Urban Development and Economic Coordinator in the mayor's office from 1954 to 1962.

6. Ibid., p. 25.

7. Philadelphia City Planning Commission, *Comprehensive Plan: The Physical Development Plan for the City of Philadelphia* (Philadelphia, 1960), p. ix.

8. A graphic description of the Better Philadelphia Exhibition of 1947 is contained in Lowe, *Cities in a Race with Time*, pp. 222–323.

9. Transcript of 1977 interview with Robert Mitchell conducted by Walter Phillips (Urban Archives Collection, Temple University, Philadelphia).

10. Petshek, *The Challenge of Urban Reform*, pp. 100–1.

11. Paul Boyer, *Urban Masses and Moral Order in America, 1820–1920* (Cambridge, Mass.: Harvard University Press, 1978), p. 224.

12. Ibid., p. 235.

13. Ibid., p. 237.

14. Harvey Shepard, "Municipal Housekeeping in Europe and America," *American City* (May 1912) quoted in Boyer, *Ibid.*, p. 264.

15. Catherine Bauer, quoted in John Bauman, "Visions of a Postwar City: A Perspective on Urban Planning in Philadelphia and the Nation, 1942–1945," *Urbanism Past and Present* 6, no. 1 (Winter/Spring 1980/81) p. 4.

16. Conrad Weiler, *Philadelphia: Neighborhoods, Authority, and the Urban Crisis* (New York: Praeger, 1974), pp. 104–5.

17. Petshek, *The Challenge of Urban Reform*, p. 72.

18. Philadelphia City Planning Commission, *Re-evaluation of the 1960 Comprehensive Plan for Philadelphia* (Philadelphia, January 1979), p. 29.

19. William Rafsky, "Urban Renewal in Philadelphia," in Stanley Newman, ed., *The Politics of Utopia: Toward America's Third Century* (proceedings of a lecture series sponsored by the Temple University Political Science Department, April/May 1975), p. III–7.

20. Sam Bass Warner, *The Private City* (Philadelphia, University of Pennsylvania Press, 1968), p. 206.

21. Minutes of the CCCP, Urban Archives Collection, Temple University. See also John Bauman, *Public Housing, Race and Renewal: Urban Planning in Philadelphia, 1920–1974* (Philadelphia: Temple University Press, 1987), p. 100.

22. Philadelphia City Planning Commission, *Comprehensive Plan*, p. 78.

23. Ibid., p. 75.

24. Joseph Clark, "To Come to the Aid of Their Cities," in Ray Ginger, ed., *Modern American Cities* (Chicago: University of Chicago Press, 1969), p. 210.

25. Brown and Gilbert, *Planning Municipal Investment*, pp. 83–84.

26. Warner, *The Private City*, p. 208.

27. Memorandum from Petshek to Bacon dated June 5, 1961. Personal papers of Kirk Petshek, Urban Archives Collection, Temple University.

28. "Capital Program Priorities," memorandum from the City Economist dated March 24, 1961. Personal papers of Kirk Petshek, *Ibid.*, p. 4.

29. Petshek, *The Challenge of Urban Reform*, p. 110.

30. Brown and Gilbert, *Planning Municipal Investment*, p. 23.

31. Edmund Bacon, "Planning, Architecture, and Politics in Philadelphia" (Russell Van Nest Black Memorial Lecture delivered at Cornell University, Ithaca, New York, April 24, 1973).

32. Transcript of 1977 interview with Edmund Bacon conducted by Walter Phillips (Urban Archives Collection, Temple University).

33. Vukan Vuchic and W. Bruce Allen, *Transportation*, Task Force Report of the Philadelphia: Past, Present, and Future Project (University of Pennsylvania; Center for Philadelphia Studies, 1982), p. 3.

34. Weiler, *Philadelphia*, p. 169.

35. Text of luncheon address by Paul Davidoff, Minutes of the CCCP, February 1965 (Urban Archives Collection, Temple University).

36. Philadelphia City Planning Commission, *Re-evaluation*, pp. 38–40.

37. J. David Greenstone and Paul Peterson, *Race and Authority in Urban Politics: Community Participation and the War on Poverty* (Chicago: University of Chicago Press, 1973), p. 26.

38. John H. Strange, "Blacks and Philadelphia Politics: 1953–1966," in Miriam Ershkowitz and Joseph Zikmund, eds., *Black Politics in Philadelphia* (New York: Basic Books, 1973), pp. 109–44.

39. Greenstone and Peterson, p. 28.

40. Elliott White, "Articulateness, Political Mobility, and Conservatism: An analysis of the Philadelphia Antipoverty Election," in Ershkowitz and Zikmund, *Black Politics*, p. 201; also Kenneth Clark and Jeanette Hopkins, *A Relevant War Against Poverty* (New York: Harper & Row, 1970), p. 165.

41. Strange, "Blacks and Philadelphia Politics."

42. *Philadelphia Evening Bulletin*, January 20, 1970, p. 1.

43. William Cutler, "The Persistent Dualism, Centralization and Decentralization in Philadelphia, 1954–1975," in William Cutler and Howard Gillette, eds., *The Divided Metropolis: Social and Spatial Dimensions of Philadelphia 1800–1975* (Westport, Conn.: Greenwood Press, 1980), p. 273.

44. Pennsylvania Economy League, *An Evaluation of the Capital Programming Process for the City of Philadelphia, With Emphasis on the Recreation/Culture Function* (Philadelphia, March 1984), p. 33.


# CHAPTER 3

1. See, for example, Robert Coughlin, Kenneth Bieri and Thomas Plaut, "The Distribution of Social Service Facilities within the City of Philadelphia," (Philadelphia; Discussion Paper no. 93 Regional Science Research Institute, December 1976.)

2. Philadelphia City Planning Commission, *Philadelphia: A City of Neighborhoods*, (Philadelphia, 1976). See also Peter Muller, Kenneth Meyer and Roman Cybriwsky, *Metropolitan Philadelphia: A Study of Conflicts and Social Cleavages* (Cambridge, Mass.: Ballinger, 1976), p. 12.

3. Of the 364 census tracts located within the city, I aggregated a total of 306 into my 104 neighborhoods, excluding the other 57 for the following reasons: (1) the 12 tracts that constitute the central business district, because the study focuses on neighborhood change and is not concerned with downtown development, (2) 32 tracts defined as "nonresidential" because they had fewer than 1000 residents in the 1970 census, (3) 13 tracts whose boundaries changed so dramatically between the 1950 and 1980 censuses as to make comparisons across decades impossible.

4. Muller *et al*, *Metropolitan Philadelphia*, p. 1.

5. The index of dissimilarity measures the percentages of either black or white population that would have to move to a tract dominated by the other race in order to achieve racial balance. Reported for Philadelphia in Ira Goldstein and William Yancey, "Projects, Blacks, and Public Policy: The Historical

Ecology of Public Housing in Philadelphia" (unpublished paper, Philadelphia: Temple University Institute for Public Policy Studies, 1983).

6. To convert each project's price tag into constant dollars, I assumed that the dollars had been spent in the year in which the project was completed, even though in some cases construction activity extended over a longer period. Tallying expenditures according to the completion data seemed to be the best way to reflect each project's actual value to the neighborhood. It is only when completed that the project becomes visible as an asset to the neighborhood; while still under construction, it may be either invisible or even disruptive to residents.

7. For use of the coefficient of variation in studies similar to this one, see Robert Lineberry, *Equality and Urban Policy: The Distribution of Municipal Public Services* (Beverly Hills: Sage, 1977), p. 107, and also John Boyle and David Jacobs, "The Intracity Distribution of Services: A Multivariate Analysis," *American Political Science Review* 76, no. 2 (June 1982) p. 375.

8. Cut-off points for each of the 3 income categories differed from decade to decade. For example, the neighborhoods in the "lowest income" category in the 1950s are those whose median income in the 1950 census fell below $3,000, while the neighborhoods in that same category in the 1960s had median incomes up to $4,950 in 1960. The cut-off point for the "lowest income" category in 1970 was $6,610.

9. David Lyon, "Capital Spending: The Neighborhoods of Philadelphia," *Business Review of the Federal Reserve Bank of Philadelphia* (1970), p. 17.

10. J. David Greenstone and Paul Peterson, *Race and Authority in Urban Politics: Community Participation and the War on Poverty* (Chicago: University of Chicago Press, 1973), p. 28.

11. Lineberry, *Equality and Urban Policy*, p. 125.

12. Interview with Barbara Kaplan, Director of the Philadelphia City Planning Commission, March 1984.

13. Philadelphia City Planning Commission, *Capital Program 1974 to 1979* (Philadelphia, 1974), pp. 96–97.

14. Susan Fainstein *et al.*, *Restructuring the City: The Political Economy of Urban Redevelopment* (New York: Longman, 1983).

15. Ibid., p. 259.

16. Kirk Petshek, *The Challenge of Urban Reform* (Philadelphia: Temple University Press, 1973), p. 141.

17. Bryan Jones, "Distributional Considerations in Models of Government Service Provision," *Urban Affairs Quarterly*, 12, no. 3 (March 1977) pp. 310, 307.

18. William Baer, "Just What is an Urban Service Anyway?" *Journal of Politics* 47 (November 1985) p. 891.

# CHAPTER 4

1. Angus Campbell, Phillip Converse, and Willard Rodgers, *The Quality of American Life* (New York: Russell Sage, 1976), p. 234.

2. Mark Fried, "Residential Attachment: Sources of Residential and Community Satisfaction," *Journal of Social Issues* 38, pp. 107–19.

3. See, for example, Paul Wendt, "Theory of Urban Land Value," *Journal of Land Economics* 33 (1957) pp. 228–40; James Barr, "City Size, Land Rent, and the Supply of Public Goods," *Regional and Urban Economics* 2 (1972) pp. 67–108; Daniel Kohlhepp and Charles Ingene, "The Effects of Municipal Services and Local Taxes on Housing Values," *Journal of American Real Estate and Urban Economics Association* 17 (1979) pp. 318–43; John Quigley, "Local Residential Mobility and Local Government Policy," in W. A. V. Clark and Eric Moore, eds., *Residential Mobility and Public Policy* (Beverly Hills: Sage, 1980), pp. 39–55.

4. See, for example, Jerome Rothenberg, "Urban Renewal Programs," in Robert Dorfman, ed., *Measuring the Benefits of Government Investment* (Washington, DC: Brookings Institution, 1965), pp. 292–341; Robert Lind, "Spatial Equilibrium, The Theory of Rents, and the Measurement of Benefits from Public Programs," *Quarterly Journal of Economics* 87 (1974) pp. 188–207; David Pines and Yoram Weiss, "Land Improvement Projects and Land Values," *Journal of Urban Economics* 3 (1976) pp. 1–13; A. Mitchell Polinsky and Steven Shavell, "Amenities and Property Values in a Model of an Urban Area," *Journal of Public Economics* 5 (1976) pp. 119–29; Stanislaw Czamanski, "Effects of Public Investments on Urban Land Values," *Journal of the American Institute of Planners* 32 (July 1968) pp. 207–14; David Lyon, "The Spatial Distribution and Impact of Public Facility Expenditures" (unpublished Ph.D. dissertation, University of California, Berkeley, 1970); S. F. Weiss, T. G. Donnelly, and E. J. Kaiser, "Land Values and Land Development Influence Factors: An Analytical Approach for Examining Policy Alternatives, *"Land Economics* (May 1966) pp. 230–3; Joseph Berechman, "Examination of the Efficient Allocation of Urban Public Facilities" (unpublished Ph.D. dissertation, University of Pennsylvania, Philadelphia, 1973).

5. Gideon Sjoberg, *The Preindustrial City* (New York: Free Press, 1960), pp. 98–99.

6. Charles Tiebout, "A Pure Theory of Local Expenditures," *Journal of Political Economy* 64 (October 1956) pp. 416–24.

7. Douglas Diamond and George Tolley, eds., *The Economics of Urban Amenities* (New York: Academic Press, 1982).

8. Wallace Oates, "The Effects of Property Taxes and Local Public Spending on Property Values: An Empirical Study of Tax Capitalization and the Tiebout Hypothesis," *Journal of Political Economy* 77 (1969) pp. 957–71.

9. Henry Pollakowski, "The Effects of Property Taxes and Local Public Spending on Property Values: A Comment and Further Results," *Journal of Political Economy* 81 (1973) pp. 995–1003; Kohlhepp and Ingene, "The Effects of Municipal Services;" Mathew Edel and Eliot Scalar, "Taxes, Spending, and Property Values: Supply Adjustment in a Tiebout/Oates Model," *Journal of Political Economy* 78, (1970) pp. 92–98; Richard Gustely, "Local Taxes, Expenditures, and Urban Housing: A Reassessment of the Evidence," *Southern Economic Journal* 42 (April 1976) pp. 659–65.

10. Albert Church, "The Effects of Local Government Expenditure and Property Taxes on Investment," *Journal of the American Real Estate and Urban Economics Association* (1981) pp. 165–77.

11. American Society of Planning Officials, *Local Capital Improvements and Development Management: Literature Synthesis* (report commissioned by the Office of Policy Development and Research, U.S. Department of Housing and Urban Development, Washington, D.C., July 1977), p. 47.

12. Edmund Bacon (then Managing Director of the Philadelphia Housing Authority), "Statement before the Philadelphia Real Estate Board," dated January 27, 1941. Personal papers of Edmund Bacon (Urban Archives Collection, Temple University, Philadelphia).

13. Kirk Petshek, *The Challenge of Urban Reform* (Philadelphia: Temple University Press, 1973), pp. 138–41.

14. Philadelphia City Planning Commission, *Comprehensive Plan: The Physical Development Plan for the City of Philadelphia,* (Philadelphia, 1960), p. 15.

15. Philadelphia City Planning Commission, *Re-evaluation of the 1960 Comprehensive Plan for Philadelphia* (Philadelphia, January 1979), p. 79.

16. Memorandum from Kirk Petshek to William Rafsky dated February 24, 1961. Personal papers of Kirk Petshek (Urban Archives Collection, Temple University, Philadelphia).

17. The accuracy of this census item has been questioned by some researchers who believe that owner-occupiers systematically underestimate the true value of their properties. If such a systematic bias does exist in the data, it is relatively unimportant for my purposes, since my focus is on the magnitude and direction of change in this figure over time, not on its absolute value in any given census year.

18. Sandra Featherman, *The Future of Public Education in Philadelphia*, Task Force Report of the Philadelphia: Past, Present, and Future Project (University of Pennsylvania; Center for Philadelphia Studies, 1982), p. 5.

19. Albert Hirschman, *The Strategy of Economic Development* (New Haven: Yale University Press, 1958).

20. Bernard Frieden and Marshall Kaplan, *The Politics of Neglect: Urban Aid from Model Cities to Revenue Sharing* (Cambridge, Mass.: MIT Press, 1975), p. 5.

21. Paul Dommel, V. Bach, S. Liebschutz, and L. Rubinowitz, *Targeting Community Development*, 3d report of the Brookings Institution Monitoring Study of the CDBG Program (prepared under contract with the U.S. Department of Housing and Urban Development, Washington, DC, January 1980) pp. 22–23.

22. Jane Jacobs, *The Death and Life of Great American Cities* (New York: Random House, 1961), p. 280.

23. Peter Rossi, *Why Families Move* (New York: Free Press, 1955), p. 85.

24. David Varady, "Determinants of Residential Mobility Decisions: The Role of Government Services in Relation to Other Factors," *Journal of the American Planning Association* 49 (Spring 1983) p. 193.

25. Julian Wolpert, Anthony Mumphrey, and John Seley, "Metropolitan Neighborhoods: Participation and Conflict over Change," Resource Paper No. 16 (Association of American Geographers, Washington, D.C., 1972); John Seley, *The Politics of Public Facility Planning* (Lexington, Mass.: Lexington Books, 1983); Michael O'Hare, "Not on My Block You Don't: Facility Siting and the Strategic Importance of Compensations," *Public Policy* (Fall 1977) pp. 407–458.

26. This is the argument put forward by Herbert Gans in *The Urban Villagers* (New York: Free Press, 1962). Gans's study of Boston's West End was followed by numerous other studies of inner city neighborhoods in the 1960s and 1970s, emphasizing the psychological ties as well as the economic necessities that have bound many lower- and lower-middle-income families to their neighborhoods. See, for example, Marc Fried, "Grieving for a Lost Home," in

James Q. Wilson, ed., *Urban Renewal: The Record and the Controversy*, (Cambridge, Mass.: MIT Press, 1967), pp. 359–79; Paul Levy, *Queen Village: The Eclipse of Community* (Philadelphia; Institute for the Study of Civic Values, 1978).

27. On the existence of racially segmented housing markets in American cities, see Luigi Laurenti, *Property Value and Race* (Berkeley: University of California Press, 1960), and Harvey Molotch, *Managed Integration: Dilemmas of Doing Good in the City* (Berkeley: University of California Press, 1972).

28. Varady, "Determinants of Residential Mobility," pp. 189–90.

29. David Harvey, *Social Justice and the City* (Baltimore: Johns Hopkins University Press, 1973); *The Limits to Capital* (Chicago: University of Chicago Press, 1982); John Logan and Harvey Molotch, *Urban Fortunes* (Berkeley: University of California Press, 1987).

30. For a discussion of lead vs. lag theories of investment in public facilities see Michael Pagano and Richard Moore, *Cities and Fiscal Choices: A New Model of Urban Public Investment* (Durham: Duke University Press, 1985), pp. 92–101.

## CHAPTER 5

1. George Sternlieb, "The Post Shelter Society," *The Public Interest* 57 (Fall 1979) pp. 39–47.

2. Sandra Featherman, *The Future of Public Education in Philadelphia*, Task Force Report of the Philadelphia: Past, Present and Future Project (University of Pennsylvania, Center for Philadelphia Studies, 1982), p. 4. Philadelphia's enrollment trend conforms to national trends; enrollment in U.S. public schools peaked in 1971–72 and has been declining ever since. See David Reynolds, "School Budget Retrenchment and Locational Conflict: Crisis in Local Democracy," in Andrew Kirby, Paul Kantor, and Steven Pinch, eds., *Public Service Provision and Urban Development* (New York: St. Martin's Press, 1984).

3. Theodore Lowi, "The State of the City in the Second Republic," in John Blair and David Nachmias, eds., *Fiscal Retrenchment and Urban Policy* (Beverly Hills: Sage, 1979), p. 53.

4. W. H. Brown and C. E. Gilbert, *Planning Municipal Investment: A Case Study of Philadelphia* (Philadelphia: University of Pennsylvania Press, 1961), p. 25.

5. Robert Coughlin and Charles Pitts, "The Capital Programming Process," *Journal of the American Institute of Planners* 26 (August 1960) pp. 237–38.

6. Ibid., p. 239.

7. Brown and Gilbert, *Planning Municipal Investment*, pp. 107–9.

8. Kirk Petshek, *The Challenge of Urban Reform* (Philadelphia: Temple University Press, 1973), p. 287.

9. *Germantown Courier,* June 29, 1983, p. 17.

10. Transcript of 1977 interview with Robert Mitchell conducted by Walter Phillips (Urban Archives Collection, Temple University, Philadelphia).

11. Philadelphia City Planning Commission, *Summary of Recreation Inventory and Trends from 1968–1978* (Philadelphia, March 1979).

12. Richard Krauss, *Recreation Needs Assessment and Marketing Analysis of Leisure Services in Philadelphia* (report commissioned by the Commissioner of Recreation, City of Philadelphia, February, 1983), p. IV/41.

13. Ibid., p. V/29.

14. Joseph Coleman (President of City Council), "City Council is not Profligate," letter to the editor, *Philadelphia Inquirer,* May 21, 1982.

15. *Philadelphia Inquirer,* January 7, 1983.

16. *Philadelphia Inquirer,* April 13, 1983.

17. Pennsylvania Economy League, *An Evaluation of the Capital Programming Process for the City of Philadelphia with Emphasis on the Recreation/Culture Function* (Philadelphia, March 1984), p. 40.

18. City Council President Joseph Coleman, quoted in the *Philadelphia Inquirer,* May 22, 1985.

19. *Philadelphia Inquirer,* June 16, 1986.

20. For a colorful description of this powerful business manager, see Peter Binzen, *Whitetown USA* (New York: Vintage Books, 1970), pp. 274–6.

21. Minutes of the CCCP, 1962 Urban Archives Collection, Temple University, Philadelphia.

22. Greater Philadelphia Movement, *A Citizen's Study of Public Education in Philadelphia,* part B (Philadelphia, 1962), p. 67.

23. Conrad Weiler, *Neighborhood, Authority, and the Urban Crisis* (New York: Praeger Publishers, 1974), p. 80.

24. Transcript of 1977 interview with Graham Finney conducted by Walter Phillips (Urban Archives Collection, Temple University, Philadelphia). Finney is still active in capital planning. He currently holds the post of chair of the Philadelphia City Planning Commission.

25. Ibid.

26. Weiler, *Philadelphia*, p. 92.

27. Binzen, *Whitetown USA*, p. 297.

28. Reynolds, "School Budget Retrenchment." In the same volume see also Rex Honey and David Sorenson, "Jurisdictional Benefits and Local Costs: The Politics of School Closings," pp. 114–30.

29. *Philadelphia Inquirer*, March 23, 1983.

30. Wilbur Thompson, "Toward A Strategy for Central City Depopulation," in Edward Hanten, Mark Kasoff and F. Stevens Redburn, eds., *New Directions for the Mature Metropolis* (Cambridge, Mass.: Schenkman, 1980), pp. 142–53. See also James Heilbrun, "On the Theory and Policy of Neighborhood Consolidation," *Journal of the American Planning Association* 45 (October 1979) pp. 417–27.

31. Robert Coughlin, Kenneth Bieri, and Thomas Plaut, "The Distribution of Social Service Facilities Within the City of Philadelphia," Discussion Paper No. 93 (Regional Science Research Institute, Philadelphia, December 1976), p. 1. For a related discussion, see Jennifer Wolch, "The Residential Location Behavior of Service-Dependent Households," (unpublished Ph.D. dissertation, Princeton University, 1979). Also A. N. White, "Accessibility and Public Facility Location," *Economic Geography* 55 (1979) pp. 18–35.

32. Michael Dear, "The Public City," in W. A. V. Clark and Eric Moore, eds., *Residential Mobility and Public Policy* (Beverly Hills: Sage, 1980), p. 231.

33. John Seley, *The Politics of Public Facility Planning* (Lexington, Mass.: Lexington Books, 1983); Michael Dear and S. M. Taylor, *Not On Our Street: Community Attitudes to Mental Health Care* (London: Methuen, 1982); S. M. Taylor, G. B. Hall, R. C. Hughes, and M. J. Dear, "Predicting Community Reaction to Mental Health Facilities," in *Journal of the American Planning Association* 50 (Winter 1984) pp. 36–47; Gabriel Stuart and Jennifer Wolch, "Spillover Effects of Human Service Facilities in a Racially Segmented Housing Market," *Journal of Urban Economics* 16 (1984) pp. 339–50.

34. Michael Pagano and Richard Moore, *Cities and Fiscal Choices: A New Model of Urban Public Investment* (Durham: Duke University Press, 1985), pp. 52–53.


## CHAPTER 6

1. Indeed, one critique of these studies complained that too many of them have included downtown and other nonresidential neighborhoods in their samples, thereby distorting the correlations between expenditures and neighborhood characteristics. This particular critique argued that once the nonresidential areas are excluded from such studies, it becomes clearer that poor minority communities receive lower levels of expenditures than more affluent neighborhoods. Fredric Bolotin and David Cingranelli, "Equity and Urban Policy: The Underclass Hypothesis Revisited," *Journal of Politics* 45 (February 1983) pp. 209–19.

2. Clarence Stone, *Economic Growth and Neighborhood Discontent: System Bias in the Urban Renewal Program of Atlanta* (Chapter Hill: University of North Carolina Press, 1976); John Mollenkopf, *The Contested City* (Princeton: Princeton University Press, 1983); Susan Fainstein et al., *Restructuring the City: The Political Economy of Urban Redevelopment* (New York: Longman, 1983).

3. Jeanne Lowe, *Cities in a Race with Time: Progress and Poverty in America's Renewing Cities* (New York: Random House, 1967), p. 351.

4. Kirk Petshek, *The Challenge of Urban Reform* (Philadelphia: Temple University Press, 1973), pp. 218–19.

5. D. Kelly O'Day, *Philadelphia Infrastructure Survey*, report prepared for Philadelphia; Past, Present, and Future Project (University of Pennsylvania Center for Philadelphia Studies, Fall 1981), p. 19.

6. *Annual Report of the Director of Finance, City of Philadelphia*, various years.

7. For a succinct and readable description of the municipal bond market see Alberta Sbragia, "Politics, Local Government, and the Municipal Bond Market," in Sbragia, ed., *The Municipal Money Chase: The Politics of Local Government Finance* (Boulder: Westview Press, 1983), pp. 67–112. For a detailed discussion of revenue bonds see Alan Steiss, *Local Government Finance: Capital Facilities Planning and Debt Administration* (Lexington: Lexington Books, 1975), chapter 8.

8. U.S. Department of the Treasury, *Report on the Fiscal Impact of the Economic Stimulus Package on 48 Large Urban Governments*, (Washington, DC, 1978).

9. Albert Gaudiosi, quoted in Lenora Berson, "Philadelphia Evolution of Economic Urban Planning, 1945–1980," in John Raines, Lenora Berson and David Gracie, eds., *Community and Capital in Conflict* (Philadelphia: Temple University Press, 1982), p. 191.

10. George Peterson, "Capital Spending and Capital Obsolescence: The Outlook for Cities," in Roy Bahl, ed., *The Fiscal Outlook for Cities: Implications of a National Urban Policy* (Syracuse: Syracuse University Press, 1978), p. 60.

11. W. H. Brown and C. E. Gilbert, *Planning Municipal Investment: A Case Study of Philadelphia* (Philadelphia: University of Pennsylvania Press, 1961), pp. 83–84.

12. Michael Pagano and Richard Moore, *Cities and Fiscal Choices: A New Model of Urban Public Investment* (Durham: Duke University Press, 1985), p. 89.

13. Ibid., p. 58.

14. Margaret Corwin and Judith Getzels, "Capital Expenditures: Causes and Controls," in Robert Burchell and David Listokin, eds., *Cities Under Stress: The Fiscal Crisis of Urban America* (New Brunswick, NJ: Rutgers University Center for Urban Policy Research, 1981), p. 389.

15. Deborah Matz and John Petersen, "Trends in the Fiscal Condition of Cities: 1980 to 1982" (staff study prepared for the Joint Economic Committee, 97th Congress, 2d session, September 1982).

16. U.S. Bureau of the Census, *City Government Finances in 1983–84*, series GF84, no. 4. (U.S. Government Printing Office, 1985), pp. 94, 102.

17. See, for example, George Pidot and Michael Goetz, *The Public Purse*, report of the Public Finance Task Force of the Philadelphia: Past, Present, and Future Project (University of Pennsylvania Center for Philadelphia Studies, Philadelphia, 1981).

18. Matz and Petersen, "Trends in the Fiscal Condition of Cities."

19. National League of Cities and U.S. Conference of Mayors, *Capital Budgeting and Infrastructure in American Cities: An Initial Assessment* (Washington, DC, April 1983), p. iii.

20. George Peterson and Mary John Miller, *Financing Public Infrastructure: Policy Options* (Washington, DC: Public Technology, Inc. 1982), p. 29.

21. Edwin Wolf, *Philadelphia: Portrait of an American City* (Harrisburg, PA: Stackpole Books, 1975), pp. 210–11.

22. Ibid., p. 237.

23. Stephen Feldman, *Energy In Philadelphia: The Present and the Future,* report of the Energy Task Force of the Philadelphia: Past, Present, and Future Project (University of Pennsylvania Center for Philadelphia Studies, 1981), pp. 6–10. See also Kristin Dawkins, "Reorganizing PGW," *Neighborhood Newsletter,* (Institute for the Study of Civic Values, Philadelphia, March 1983).

24. *Philadelphia Inquirer,* October 10, 1983.

25. *Philadelphia Inquirer,* January 28, 1983.

26. *Philadelphia Inquirer,* March 24, 1983.

27. For a good general discussion of the ways in which the requirements of the capital market constrain public authorities' options, see Alberta Sbragia, "Borrowing to Build: Private Money and Public Welfare," *International Journal of Health Services* 9 (1979) pp. 207–26.

28. On sale/leasebacks and other approaches to financing public works see Roger Vaughan, *Rebuilding America,* vol. 2: Financing Public Works in the 1980s (Washington, D.C.: Council of State Planning Agencies, 1983); Government Finance Research Center, *Building Prosperity: Financing Public Infrastructure for Economic Development* (Chicago: Municipal Finance Officers Association, 1983); John Petersen and Wesley Hough, *Creative Capital Financing for State and Local Governments* (Chicago: Municipal Finance Officers Association, 1983).

29. *Philadelphia Inquirer,* April 15, 1985.


# CHAPTER 7


1. James Reichley, *The Art of Government: Reform and Organization Politics in Philadelphia* (New York: Fund for the Republic, 1959).

2. Roger Friedland and William Bielby, "The Power of Business in the City," in Terry Clark, ed., *Urban Policy Analysis* (Beverly Hills: Sage, 1981), p. 145.

3. Thomas Boast, "Urban Resources, the American Capital Market, and Federal Programs," in Douglas Ashford, ed., *National Resources and Urban Policy* (New York: Methuen, 1980), pp. 77, 80.

4. Paul Kantor and Stephen David, "The Political Economy of Change in Urban Budgetary Politics: A Framework for Analysis and A Case Study," *British Journal of Political Science* 13 (1983) p. 281.

5. Theodore Lowi, "The State of Cities in the Second Republic," in John Blair and David Nachmias, eds., *Fiscal Retrenchment and Urban Policy* (Beverly Hills: Sage, 1979), pp. 43–54.

6. Martin Shefter, "New York City's Fiscal Crisis," *The Public Interest* 48 (Summer 1977) pp. 125, 119.

7. Kirk Petshek, *The Challenge of Urban Reform* (Philadelphia: Temple University Press, 1973), pp. 87–90.

8. Annmarie Hauck Walsh, *The Public's Business: The Politics and Practices of Governmental Corporations* (Cambridge, Mass.: MIT Press, 1978), pp. 234–55.

9. James Bennett and Thomas DiLorenzo, *Underground Government: The Off-Budget Public Sector* (Washington, DC: Cato Institute, 1983). Another critical account is Diana Henriques, *The Machinery of Greed: Public Authority Abuse and What To Do About It (Lexington, Mass.: Lexington Books, 1986).*

10. Bennet and DiLorenzo, *Underground Government*, p. 41.

11. Roger Friedland, Frances Fox Piven, and Robert Alford, "Political Conflict, Urban Structure and the Fiscal Crisis," in Douglas Ashford, ed., *Comparing Public Policies* (Beverly Hills: Sage, 1978).

12. Alberta Sbragia, "Politics, Local Government, and the Municipal Bond Market," in Sbragia, ed., *The Municipal Money Chase: The Politics of Local Government Finance* (Boulder: Westview Press, 1983), p. 100.

13. Heywood Sanders, "Politics and Urban Public Facilities," in Royce Hanson, ed., *Perspectives on Urban Infrastructure* (Washington, DC: National Academy Press, 1984), p. 167.

14. John Logan and Harvey Molotch, *Urban Fortunes* (Berkeley: University of California Press, 1987), pp. 220ff.

# Index